48 Hours to Hammelburg

At 8.30 the wind suddenly died down and visibility cleared almost magically. To his consternation, Waters now saw that over twenty enemy tanks were crawling like squat, evil, khaki-coloured bugs to the west of his position. He was cut off from the rear! Five minutes later the number had risen to thirty-nine. And there seemed no end to the bastards. When he had counted over eighty enemy vehicles, he gave up counting. It was pretty obvious what had happened to the forward positions under the weight of such a massive German attack. Grimly Waters bit his bottom lip and considered for a moment what he should do next.

Charles Whiting

48 Hours to Hammelburg

Arrow Books

Arrow Books Limited
3 Fitzroy Square, London W 1 P 6 J D

An imprint of the Hutchinson Publishing Group

London Melbourne Sydney Auckland
Wellington Johannesburg and agencies
throughout the world

First published in Great Britain 1979

© Charles Whiting 1970

Made and printed in Great Britain
by The Anchor Press Ltd
Tiptree, Essex

ISBN 0 09 919990 4

Contents

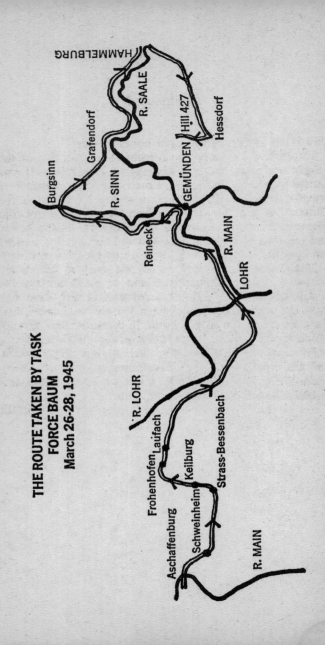

THE ROUTE TAKEN BY TASK
FORCE BAUM
March 26-28, 1945

(HAMMELBURG)

R. SAALE

Grafendorf

Burgsinn

R. SINN

GEMÜNDEN   Hill 427

Hessdorf

Reineck

R. MAIN

LOHR

R. LOHR

Frohenhofen Laufach

Keilburg

Aschaffenburg

Schweinheim

Strass-Bessenbach

R. MAIN

Foreword

This is the story of forty-eight hours of war.

It tells how in the course of those two days one of the boldest and most exciting missions of World War II was carried out far behind the German lines by a handful of brave American soldiers. Yet in spite of having all the elements of a great popular adventure, it is a story that has never been told before in detail because of the power and position of the man who ordered the mission carried out (and he has been dead over a quarter of a century).

This is the first attempt to tell the story in full detail. Naturally, after so much time and so much secrecy the details were hard to find, but there are still men alive who know the truth. They range from Private to General, and I owe my thanks to them all; but, in particular, to Colonels Matthews and Lacey, former prisoners in the Hammelburg POW camp, General von Goeckel, its last commandant, and Sir Kenneth Strong, Eisenhower's chief of Intelligence. To them—and all the others who have helped me in half a dozen countries—thank you.

—C.W.

"It takes 16,000 dead to train a major-general"
Marshal Joffre

Introduction

On a dark March night one month before the end of World War II, some 307 American soldiers in 53 vehicles waited in tense expectancy beside a railway bridge that crossed the German River Main. Before them the roar of the artillery barrage grew ever louder and the darkness was illuminated momentarily by the bursting of the shells, which were now beginning to fall on the German positions. Urgent red flares hissed into the sky. Somewhere a machine gun commenced its chattering. It was answered by the rapid frightening burr of an enemy Spandau. The attack was about to begin.

That night the mixed tank and half-track force waiting on that railway bridge just south of the town of Aschaffenburg was about to start on one of the strangest missions of the whole long, bloody war. Under the command of tall, brawny Captain Baum, a red-haired, pink-complexioned former tailor's cutter from New York City, the force was to cross the river, penetrate through sixty miles of enemy territory held by an estimated three divisions, capture the German POW camp above the little town of Hammelburg and rescue the thousand-odd American officers held prisoner there. If the mission was successful, the force was then to return with its half-tracks loaded with the prisoners through the same sixty enemy-held miles!

But now, on this dark March night a quarter of a century ago, the expedition did not think of what lay before them. Their immediate concern was that the combat command to which they belonged—cigar-chewing Lieutenant Colonel Creighton Abrams' 4th Armored Division's Combat Command B—would be able to battle its way through the village of Schweinheim (soon to be called "Bazooka

City" by the GI's) and free a path for them so that they could get the expedition started.

"It was dusk when the battalion commander was heard on the radio picking up his companies," recalls Corporal William W. Smith, who drove a Sherman that night. "Then about thirty minutes later we heard him call again and give our company commander his orders. He was to attack this small town two miles away to let the task force through. The town was reported not to have too much resistance, *but when you hear that, watch out!*

"The order to 'turn 'em over' made me feel creepy, because I had never been on a night attack before. I warmed up the engine and drove my tank to its usual position. As soon as the artillery fire lifted, we started to move in."

The lead American Sherman was stopped by a direct hit within a hundred yards of the German village nestling between two large hills east of the railway bridge where Baum waited impatiently to start on his impossible mission. Then all hell broke loose. It seemed as if the Germans had been waiting for Abrams to attack them. The still night was ripped apart by the volume of enemy fire. Red and white tracer zipped through the sky like myriad angry hornets. German Schmeisser machine pistols hissed viciously, to be answered by the slower chatter of the American grease guns. Everywhere the German bazooka-men fired their Panzerfausts at the advancing U.S. tanks. A second Sherman went up in flames, bathing the scene in its fiery red light. Moments later its ammunition racks exploded, sending shells zigzagging crazily into the night sky. Men began to fall everywhere.

It was 2:30 on the morning of March 27, 1945, when the young captain from the Bronx, who had already been wounded in combat once before, received his orders to advance. He needed no urging. He had been waiting for that command since midnight. "TURN 'EM OVER!" he roared into his mouthpiece above the roar of the battle still raging on the other side of the dark, swift-flowing river. His crew, the veterans as well as the new men, responded with alacrity, almost as if they were eager to

begin this desperate mission so soon to result in death
for so many of them.

With their engines racing, they clattered in their Shermans and half-tracks through the burning village of
Schweinheim, past the knocked-out tanks and the dead
sprawled in the gutters in the extravagant postures of men
suddenly killed in combat. Their passage through the
little German village did not take them long. Soon they
left behind them the last American outposts and headed
for the country road which would take them to the river-
head town of Gemünden and the vital bridge they would
need to get them to Hammelburg. Task Force Baum was
underway. Behind them the German line closed up, effec-
tively sealing them off from the rest of the Combat Command.

Most of the men who set off on that dark March night
on an expedition which General Omar Bradley was later
to characterize as beginning "as a wild goose chase and
end[ing] as a tragedy," were never to return. Around
eight o'clock on the morning of the 27th, divisional headquarters of the 4th Armored received a laconic radio
message from Baum: "Tell air of enemy marshaling yards
at Gemünden." Later that same day he reported once
more that he had lost four medium tanks, two officers
and several enlisted men. Then the messages ceased save
for one last two-word statement at 0300 hours on the
morning of March 28: "Mission accomplished."

Thereafter there was silence.

A few days later a couple of stragglers, starved and
still shocked from their ordeal, staggered into the American lines. They were questioned and quickly sent to the
rear. At the village of Nesselrode, tankers of the 4th
Armored picked up a German newspaper abandoned on
the war-littered cobbled street. It headlined the story of
an American armored unit which had been wiped out in
savage fighting near the town of Hammelburg. At about
the same time, Reuters picked up reports from the German
radio in Berlin which stated—as printed in the London
Times of March 29, 1945—that "An American motorized

force has reached the area of Lohr on the River Main, nineteen miles east of Aschaffenburg," and later that "Fierce German counterattacks were launched which wiped out the American armoured spearhead."

The days passed and became a week. Still there was no positive news of the Baum Task Force. The 4th Armored Division crossed the River Main at Hanau and charged on through Saxony, racing against time in the futile hope that it would have the honor of capturing Berlin before the Russians. Despite the boastful, bombastic Berlin news reports, the commander of the 4th, Lieutenant General William Hoge, still hoped for his men. He had a terse message sent out to his subordinate commands: "no news of Baum." Yet he still believed that the U.S. Seventh Army, which was in process of taking over the bridgehead at Aschaffenburg, would find his lost companies.

But when by April 6 he had still received no positive news, he allowed the famous 37th Tank Battalion, then at Gotha, deep in the heart of the Reich, to report 73 of its men and four of its officers "missing in action." They were the men who had manned the Shermans of Baum's force. That same day, the 10th Armored Infantry, which had supplied the force's footsloggers, did the same for its missing 209 men and six officers. "A" Company of the 10th and "C" Company of the 37th were written off and very rapidly reconstituted from the huge, sprawling Third Army replacement depots in France, just as the man who had ordered the raid had promised Lieutenant General William Hoge they would be.

And that was just about the end of the whole affair.

Within a matter of days the war in Europe was over. The Western World indulged itself in a great orgy of celebration for a short period and then set about its business again. In Germany, the troopers of the victorious Third Army concentrated on getting drunk on looted cognac, chasing *Fräuleins* and counting the points which would take them home. In the United States the great American Public, now that victory in Europe was theirs, was in a hurry to forget the whole bloody business of war.

The few survivors of Task Force Baum, who were later liberated by their victorious comrades, were flown speedily to "Camp Lucky Strike" on the French coast, where they were given priority treatment and hurried home before ex-prisoners who had spent years in German POW camps and who had been waiting at "Lucky Strike" for weeks to get a space in the overcrowded transports returning to the States. It was almost as if—as some of the few critical observers of the sorry business thought at the time—the man who had ordered the raid wanted them out of his command as quickly as possible—*as if he wanted to forget that the Hammelburg Raid had ever even happened!*

But who was that man?

He was tall, hard-eyed General George S. Patton Jr., the darling of the great American public and according to some American military writers, one of the greatest combat generals the United States has ever produced. He was the man whose fearsome nickname, "Old Blood and Guts," even today, a quarter of a century after his death, is still a household word for most Americans. A man whose statue, adorned with his favorite twin pistols decorates the campus at West Point[1]—presumably as a spur to the ambitious young officer of today; a man who has a barracks named after him in Germany and a national day of liberation in little Luxembourg; whose life story has recently been told in a million-dollar Hollywood movie.

Why, then, did this renowned general order such an impossible undertaking, which seemed doomed to failure right from the start?

After the war, in the few months left to him to live, General Patton wrote in justification of his decision to attack the camp high up on the plateau above the little town of Hammelburg:

There were two purposes in this expedition: first to impress the Germans with the idea that we were moving due

---

[1]The Patton pistols are regarded as a holy relic at West Point where they are stored, and the film company shooting the Patton movie was refused permission to borrow them for the production.

east, whereas we intended to move due north and second to
release 900 American prisoners of war who were at Hammelburg.

Today it seems that every word of that statement was
less than accurate. But, as we shall see, it has been swallowed in all innocence hook, line, and sinker for over
twenty-odd years by the few writers who have occupied
themselves with the Hammelburg affair. Dr. Martin
Blumenson, former Army colonel and noted military historian, is typical. Writing in the reputable *Army* magazine
in 1955, he maintained in all seriousness:

Did the acton [the Hammelburg Raid] have a sound military
basis? Or was it the result of personal interest on the part
of General Patton?

The occurrence took place toward the end of March,
1945 when Patton's Third Army was through the Siegfried
Line and 30 miles beyond the Rhine River. When the 4th
Armored Division crossed the Main River and took Aschaffenburg,[2] the stage was set for the Hammelburg adventure.
[It is interesting to note that even Blumenson cannot re-
frain from calling the raid an "adventure."]

Deception is a cardinal principle of warfare. Like a good
boxer or halfback, a good general knows the value of a
well-executed feint. Ordered to turn his army to the north
from Aschaffenburg, Patton had a marvelous opportunity to
deceive the Germans. A foray to the east would disguise his
intention of swinging to the north.

A quick glance at a military map of the terrain would
soon convince Dr. Blumenson of the implausibility of his
statement. The route Baum would have to—and did—
take to get to Hammelburg was flanked on one side by
the River Main and on the other by steep hills. A determined German platoon with one single anti-tank gun
could have easily held up the two-company Baum force
on the narrow road that leads to Gemünden and then on
to Hammelburg.

If this is true, why did Patton pick Hammelburg as
his objective? Why plan a raid intended as a strategic
deception, if there was a good possibility that it would

---

[2]The town was only taken a day *after* the raid had started.

be stopped even before it got started, as it almost was at Schweinheim?

Colonel Codman, his chief aide, who was with General Patton on the day he gave his final instructions to General Manton Eddy, the commander of the corps to which the 4th Armored Division belonged, sees a far more humanitarian reason for the raid. Codman wrote in his diary that day:

> Accompanied the General on a flight across the Rhine, an impressive sight from the air. First stop, General Eddy's headquarters, where the General ordered an expedition sent to Hammelburg to liberate nine hundred American prisoners reported to be in a POW camp there. Al Stiller,[3] who now really has blood in his eye, is going with them.

But "Old Blood and Guts" had never been known for his sentiment nor for any particular humanitarian streak in his character. He spoke of himself as a man who had made many widows in his time, and once justified his constant swaggering and swearing to his nephew Fred Ayer as follows:

> In any war, a commander, no matter what his rank, has to send to sure death, nearly every day, by his own orders, a certain number of men. Some are his personal friends. All are his personal responsibility, to them as his troops and to their families. Any man with a heart would, then, like to sit down and bawl like a baby, but he can't. So he sticks out his jaw and swaggers and swears. I wish some of those pious sob sisters at home could understand something as basic at that.

Those are the words of a man who had put softness and sentiment behind him. Why should he be particularly concerned about the fate of a handful of men, who would be liberated sooner or later anyhow, when he was daily concerned with the fates of nearly three quarters of a million men who made up his Army? Why, too, would he risk sending along his old friend and favorite aide Al Stiller, of whom he would say later, after Stiller had been

---

[3] Major Alexander Stiller, Patton's other aide, who had been a tank sergeant in Patton's old outfit in World War I. We shall hear much more of him later.

reported missing in action, "No one who knows me would believe that I'd sacrifice Stiller to save my own brother"? *WHY?*

There were some, of course, who knew from the start the real reason why General George S. Patton ordered the fantastic Hammelburg raid. Stiller knew, but he died with his lips sealed. Colonel Creighton Abrams, one day to become a four-star general and commander in chief in Vietnam, knew, but he was a Patton man, cut in the same mold as the general, to whom he owed much of his meteoric rise up the military ladder. He, too, kept his mouth shut. Then there was General Hoge, a bitter, disappointed man in many ways, who had never seen his full promise realized, who had viewed inferior general officers promoted over his head because he was simply too outspoken. He also remained silent, though he had objected to the raid right from the start. And although General of the Army Omar Bradley did not know the real reason for the raid till much later—in fact, when he wrote his memoirs, he still accepted Patton's version of the story—Bradley's boss, the Supreme Commander and future President of the United States General Dwight D. Eisenhower knew. But he, too, for his own private reasons kept silent.

In short, for over twenty years the Military clamped a lid of silence over the whole sorry Hammelburg story, some to protect Patton's memory, others to protect themselves and their own part in the affair. And even today, when the truth about it is known, the Military is still reluctant to give information.

Straight-shooting, honest Omar Bradley, whom Patton duped about the Hammelburg raid as he had done on other occasions, all the same protects the reputation of his fiery, hot-tempered subordinate a quarter of a century after Patton's death; writing in reply to an inquiry on the subject that he did not have the "research staff to allow [Bradley] to help in this matter." In other words, *No comment!*

Former members of the 4th Armored Division who

are still serving in the Army pass the buck when questioned on the subject and refer the inquirer to other officers. After all, the U.S. Army is still dominated by "Patton's men"—the two major U.S. armies overseas in Germany and Vietnam both are commanded by former Third Army officers. As they say in the service, "Rank hath privileges" and if you want promotion, you've got to keep in with the wheels.

As for the family, they naturally and understandably refuse to answer queries which might impair the reputation of Patton's about whom one of his many admirers wrote in June 1945 when he returned to the States at the close of the war in Europe: *His was the return of the hero.*

In this book I have attempted to tell the true story of the Hammelburg raid carried out by Task Force Baum, of which Patton himself later admitted:

> I can say this, that throughout the campaign in Europe I know of no error I made except that of failing to send a Combat Command to take Hammelburg. Otherwise my operations were to me, strictly satisfactory.

It is an attempt to justify the memory of those men of the 10th Armored Infantry and the 37th Tank Battalion, who were sent to their deaths at the whim of a general whom Dwight Macdonald, probably Patton's most articulate critic in the States, has described as "brutal and hysterical, coarse and affected, violent and empty."

It is, then, primarily a tale of fascinating, if harebrained adventure toward the end of a great war, a tale devoted to the brief forty-eight-hour life of Baum's task force, with its two companies taking on all comers, yet becoming perceptibly weaker by the hour as tank after tank exploded in flames and man after man crumpled by the wayside of the little country roads leading to Hammelburg, never to rise again.

It is a tale of bloody fighting, culminating in a "last stand" in the Custer manner with Baum's decimated force fighting it out on the slopes of Hill 427, attacked on three sides by tanks and fanatical SS officer-cadets, with their wounded crouched in the ruins on the top of the hill and no way of escape left to them save surrender—or death.

But it is also the story of the beginning of the decline and fall of one of American's greatest fighting generals, with undertones of tragedy as the dark clouds began to gather over the head of the victorious general, George S. Patton.

To the larger public the great general is a dazzling, oversized figure, who effortlessly bends great armies of men to his indomitable will. And in truth there seems to be something heroic and unique about commanders of this kind in their prime. Yet in reality they are neither omnipotent nor omniscient. They, too, have their petty weaknesses and whims like every other man in more humble circumstances. They, too, can be malicious, mean and self-centered. Read any of the memoirs of the "great" generals of World War II, with their anxious concern for their military reputation, and it will soon be obvious.

Patton was no exception. He was primarily a man who hated. He hated Englishmen, his Allies, especially Montgomery. He hated Germans, the enemy. He hated his fellow commanders (Eisenhower: 'the best general the British have'). He hated cartoonists (especially Bill Mauldin who drew two very scruffy front-line GI's named Willy and Joe). He hated politicians[4] (all of them), Jews, shell-shocked soldiers, Russians, Communists, doctors, soldiers who neglected to wear a necktie in the front-lines, psychiatrists—in short, he was a man whose life seemed to have been motivated by pure naked hate, which as the war drew to its close gained the upper hand over him.

As Dwight Macdonald said of him in 1945 after viewing a newsreel clip of Patton addressing a crowd in Los Angeles during a visit to his boyhood environment:

These utterances of Patton are atrocities of the mind; atrocious in being communicated not to a psychoanalyst

---

[4] Once Patton told his nephew Fred Ayers: "Politicians are the worst; they'll wear their country's flag in public, but they'll use it to wipe their behinds in the caucus room, if they think it will win them a vote . . . I wish I could get some of the bastards into the front line here."

but to a great number of soldiers, civilians and school children; and atrocious as reflections of what war-making has done to the personality of Patton himself.

But perhaps Captain Baum's assessment is more charitable. Today, twenty-five years later, the man he sent to almost certain death but who survived and who still admires Patton can say, half in disgust and half in admiration: "Patton was an egomaniac, who believed in ninety per cent psychology and ten per cent killing."

Part One

The Decision

xxxxxxxxxxxxxxxxxxxxxxxxxxxxxxx

My favorite general is George S. Patton Jr. Some of our generals like Stilwell have developed a sly ability to simulate human beings. But Patton always behaves as a general should. His side arms (a brace of pearl-handled revolvers) are as clean as his tongue is foul. He wears special uniforms, which like Goering, he designs himself and which are calculated like the ox horns worn by ancient Gothic chieftains to strike terror into the enemy (and any rational person for that matter).

DWIGHT MACDONALD (1944)

Chapter 1

The night was pitch black. The moon had long since disappeared. The snow came down like a solid wall. Everywhere the narrow country road, bordered on both sides by skinny firs, began to vanish under the white blanket, as if some God on high had determined that he would blot out the scene of human misery below for good.

Still the endless column trudged on, heads bent against the snowflakes, backs bowed under the homemade packs sewn out of sugar sacks, or shoulders tilted forward as they dragged the heavily laden sleds behind them.

On this road and scores of country roads like it in western Poland in the February of 1945, hundreds of thousands of German civilians were fleeing the farms and houses they had so greedily grabbed from the beaten Poles five years before. The very young, the very old and the sick rode in horse- or ox-drawn carts or anything that could move on sleds or wheels, burrowing down deep under piles of wet hay or the great feather *Federdecken* of the German farmer. The rest walked, their feet cased in the huge, clumsy, felt winter boots issued to the soldiers on the Russian front, potato sacks over their heads with holes cut for the eyes. Here and there a marcher staggered, groaned falling to his knees, collapsed softly into the snow like some grotesque puppet whose strings had been suddenly released by the puppet master. The column did not hesitate one single second. Unseeing and unfeeling it staggered on. The first heavy iron-wheeled cart bumped over the inert figure. Then another. And another. Slowly but inevitably it was pressed deeper and deeper into the snow until finally all that was left of what had once been a human body was—if the marchers had been able to see it—a patch of dirty red gore. Time was precious then—very precious. *They* were coming!

The "they" were the Russians, *Ivan,* as the fleeing Germans called them. On January 12, 1945, taking advantage of the German preoccupation with the Battle of the Bulge, almost three million Russian soldiers, supported by mass artillery and thousands of tanks had launched a surprise attack on the fewer than a million Germans who were holding the four-hundred-mile-long eastern front. They had broken through virtually everywhere.

Now, one month later, they were heading for East Prussia, driving everything before them like the yellow hordes of Attila the Hun had done. Everywhere the German civilian population had abandoned their homes, loaded their vehicles with their most precious possessions and fled, fearing the savage vengeance the Russians were exacting everywhere for the four years of systematic Nazi brutality and sadism which the Germans had exercised during their occupation of the Soviet Motherland. That February, horror stories poured in from a thousand Polish and Prussian villages. Women dragged from their hiding places, stripped naked in the snow, raped by a score of little yellow men and finally nailed through the hands to the barrel of the *Jauchewagen,* the cart the farmers used to drain the human privies for use as manure on the fields. Men lined along a wall and their marriage rings seized from them by rapacious troopers in the simplest possible way—by slicing off their fingers! A gray-haired pastor forced from his prayers by the altar and nailed to his own cross—upside down. The stories were endless, and whether they were the creations of Dr. Goebbels' Propaganda Ministry or not no one really cared: all they knew that February was that they *must* get away before the Russians came.

But mixed up among the frightened German civilians so eager to escape from the retribution of the Russians, there were some who did not want to go west; who had to be urged on by the threats of their middle-aged guards; and who, when they fell out of the column, were swiftly dragged to one side by the ruthless white-camouflaged S.S. thugs bringing up the rear, and blasted into eternity by a brutal pistol shot in the back of the head. They were the British and American prisoners of war ("kriegies," as they called themselves—from the German for POW— *Kriegsgefangener*), who were being evacuated from the great sprawling *Oflags, Luftlags* and *Stalags*[1] of Poland and Silesia into the interior of the Reich itself. *But for what reason?*

This was the frightening question that occupied the minds of many of the Americans who found themselves in the German *Treks*[2] that February, struggling on kilometer after kilometer, starved, underweight, plagued by dysentery and pneumonia and half a score of other diseases occasioned by undernourishment. Did the Germans simply want to prevent their falling into Russian hands so that they would be unable to fight again? Or were they going to be held as hostages? If so, for what?

In the evenings when they were finally allowed to collapse in the monstrously overcrowded, ice-cold churches and schools, which were to house them for the night, floors puddled in mud, snow, urine, human feces and sometimes blood, they discussed that question endlessly.

First Lieutenant Kenneth Simmons of the U.S.A.F., for instance, who had been marching for a week from the great Stalag Luft III, with its 10,000 POW's at Sagan, records one such anxious conversation, carried out with his buddies as they crouched on the freezing concrete floor of a commandeered sugar factory:

"If there were a chance of our being liberated, the Germans would march us for a solid week, if they have to. They are holding onto us at all costs, and they must have a good reason. It wouldn't surprise me at all if they take us straight to Berlin. Maybe Hitler is going to trade the ten thousand of us for his life. *Would the U.S. agree to that, if they knew we would die otherwise?*"

Squatting there in the icy coldness of the factory, their

---

[1] Various German names for types of POW camps.
[2] German name given to the refugee columns.

breath fogging grayly in tiny clouds around their heads, with over two hundred men dying all about them, they pondered the question in morose silence.

Then another officer, haggard and unshaven, his face hollowed by suffering and exhaustion, spoke:

"Maybe they are going to take us to Berlin and scatter us all over the city. If the Germans sent a message to Allied Headquarters saying that ten thousand American and British officers were scattered all over Berlin and that all of us would be put to death if the city were bombed again, what do you think would happen then?"

"The Air Force wouldn't think of bombing Berlin if we were held as hostages," someone else agreed.

"I disagree with that," another officer interrupted. "Our country is out to win this war at all costs and nothing is going to stop them from bombing Berlin until the goons surrender. *We would simply become part of the price of victory.*"

But some of the kriegies were not prepared to simply accept their fate like that. There were a few of them among the fourteen hundred prisoners who had shuffled out of their camp at Szubin in Poland and started the long trek westward that February. They were commanded by a middle-aged colonel, Paul Goode, of the U.S. Army. Paul—or "Pop" as he was usually called by his intimates—Goode, a former instructor at West Point, was a character, whose most precious possession on the march was—of all things—a set of Scotch bagpipes which he had managed to hold onto through many a difficult situation. But after the first few days of the march, even his tremendous resolution and courage began to fail.

The weather was murderously cold[3]—so much so that when Colonel James Lockett's scarf was momentarily blown away from one ear, the kriegie's skin came off as easily as if he had suffered third-degree burns. In addition, many of Goode's men had been captured in the Battle of the Bulge a few weeks before and had been on

---

[3]It was the coldest winter for thirty years in Europe.

the move every day since then. As a result they were badly undernourished—on an average they had each lost thirty pounds—exhausted and an easy prey to disease. The wake of their column was littered with dead and dying men, left to the mercy of the SS and the gray wolves which slunk out of the Polish forests. Within a few days Goode had lost four hundred men.

Yet despite the murderous conditions, the terrible weather, the physical exhaustion of the older men, the diet of barley soup and black bread, the morale of Goode's men was amazingly high, so that every time Pop's own courage began to falter he would take a look at his men and gain new strength.

Thus, while the great majority of the POW's resolved that they would get to their destination—whatever and wherever that might be—some, the hardier souls, decided that the time had come to bid adieu to their captors and the life of a kriegie. Behind them somewhere were the Russians. Somehow they might be able to get in touch with them and be shipped back to their own army in the West.

Night after night they slipped out of their temporary accommodations into the swirling snow, telling their middle-aged guards, who were often more exhausted than the younger kriegies, that they were going "to the latrine," or simply bribing them with a few of their remaining and very precious cigarettes to "look the other way for a minute, will ya?" And then out they would plunge into the snow-filled howling night to take their chances with the SS and the wolves, hoping against hope that somehow —somewhere—they would meet the first hesitant Cossack patrols, which would mean the end of misery and the beginning of freedom.

One officer who would dearly have loved to go with them was Colonel John Waters, a handsome square-jawed 39-year-old career officer from Baltimore. John Waters had attended Johns Hopkins University for two years, majoring in arts and sciences before he decided to transfer to West Point and become a regular army officer. At the Point he had been an outstanding cadet and graduated as a second lieutenant in the Cavalry in 1931. Thereafter his career up the military ladder had been slow but steady and by the time the war had broken out he had been generally regarded by his contemporaries as an officer who was going places. That is, until he had been taken prisoner of war. Now the shabby, undernourished officer with the broad, strong military face, who was usually so quiet and reserved, cursed inwardly every morning when he noted that yet another brother officer had disappeared eastward toward the advancing Russians. He knew that the time was ideally suited for a hardy and courageous man—as he was—to escape. Yet every time he took a sly glance at Pop Goode's gray, emaciated face, he knew he had to stay behind and look after the older man. It was his bounden duty. The alternative was fairly obvious. If he took off now, Pop would be dead within the week.

Yet it was hard to have to sit on his thumbs and wait for the war to end before he could be free. He had been cut off so long from everything dear to him—his wife and children and his career. Sometimes he even imagined he was beginning to forget how they all looked and had to reassure himself by gazing for a long time at their photographs. It had been two years—two long, dreary years—since he had last been a free man with the right to do and go as he pleased. Twenty-four months of deadening, sickening routine. The POW camp with its goons, "appells,"[4] searches, combines; its petty jealousies and its intense personal friendships which bordered on the abnormal; its persistent, overpowering craving for food; and, above all, the miserable feeling of having failed because one had surrendered . . .

For youthful Colonel John Waters it had all started almost exactly two years before, on the morning of Sunday, February 14, 1943—a date that would be written forever in his memory, even a quarter of a century later when he went on to become a four-star general. On that particular morning, Waters had been commanding a part of

---

[4] Prisoner slang for guards, and parades.

the 1st Armored Regiment in Tunisia, his task being to defend a hill known as the Djebel Lessouda, a key feature on the road to the Kasserine Pass, against any attack by Rommel Panzers which were known to be somewhere in the area. Across the road some miles to the south was a similar hill, Djebel Ksaira, held by a like section of the 1st Armored.

General Fredendall, the American corps commander, had personally assigned the armored regiment to the two hills although the First's senior staff officers had protested that while the positions appeared excellent on the map, they weren't mutually supporting and were very vulnerable to encirclement. But cocky little General Fredendall, whom the American military historian Martin Blumenson has characterized as an officer who "considered himself a rough, tough customer who was going to let nothing stand in his way of winning the war even if it took all kinds of flailing of arms and bearing down," rode roughshod over their protests. He even refused to allow a reconnaissance made of the features by his own officers. So the regiment had to grin and bear it. The hills *would* be defended as the general had ordered!

This morning, however, everything seemed quiet, though Waters had an uneasy feeling that the wily Desert Fox was a bit *too* quiet. Rommel knew the American troops facing him were green. Admittedly the Americans had had some initial success against the Vichy French troops they had fought during the landings in North Force. But the French were understrength, underequipped and very definitely undermotivated, and as Waters had reminded his men after their first action: "We did very well against the scrub team. Next week we hit German troops. Do not slack off in anything. When we make a showing against *them*, you may congratulate yourselves."

Now that week had passed and there was still little sign of action from the German side. Admittedly, Rommel was sick—he couldn't sleep and suffered from blinding headaches. But Waters well knew that foxes are dangerous, desperate animals when they are sick.

Thus, as the false dawn streaked the deserted sky a

dirty ugly white that gray February morning, Colonel Waters plodded heavily up the slope of Djebel Lessouda to his observation post on its summit. A bitter sand-filled wind struck him in the face, making progress difficult. Pulling up the collar of his combat jacket and burying his chin in it, Waters struggled on. But on the summit the howling wind and biting grains of sand made it virtually impossible to see or hear very much.

For a while Waters tried to peer through the whirling gloom to the plain and road he knew to be somewhere below. But in the end he gave up and plodded back the way he had come to his tent. When he got there, the telephone was ringing. Quickly Waters snatched it from the orderly. It was his boss, Colonel Peter Hains, a dapper officer who looked more like a college lecturer than a Regular Army officer.

"What's that shooting we can hear here?" Hains asked without any preliminaries.

"What shooting?" Waters echoed.

Hains replied that it seemed to be coming from somewhere on the road to Waters' front.

Hurriedly assuring the colonel he would investigate, Waters replaced the telephone and hastened up the steep hill once more. By the light of the weak yellow sun which was now trying to break through the swirling clouds of sand, he could see the quick red flashes of the guns, and he had only to turn his head to one side to hear the distinct rumble of tank tracks. Waters sensed a nervous quickening of his blood. This was it!

Quickly he sprang into action. Running down the hill to his command post, he ordered his artillery to start firing at the prearranged targets to their front. This was the attack!

The reply came back in hurried, anxious tones. It was obvious that the officer at the other end was scared— badly scared. "The Krauts are too close, sir! We'll overshoot at this range!"

"Withdraw a couple of hundred yards then," Waters snapped impatiently. "Then you can fire at them!"

"Yessir," the artillery commander agreed. "I'll do that."

Wiping the sweat off his brow, Waters rammed down the telephone, grateful to know that he would soon receive artillery support. He didn't know that his artillery was to be overrun by the leading German units a matter of minutes later. Quickly the young colonel ordered the fifteen tanks under his command into action. Their task was simple. They were to block the German advance until he had some clarity as to the enemy's intentions. Swiftly they clattered off into the dust, eager to meet the Kraut for the first time. Like the artillery, they too would soon be disillusioned when they clashed with Rommel's veteran Panzers.

Reports of first contacts with the enemy soon started to pour in from all sides. The static went up everywhere. German fighters—mostly clipped-wing Messerschmitts—began to swoop down at four hundred miles an hour over the battlefield. Flares—red, white and green—hushed effortlessly into the morning air, calling for help, artillery and air support. Tracer bullets stitched a red pattern across the valley. Like a swarm of angry hornets, rapid artillery fire broke out on both sides of Waters' positions. This, Waters thought ruthfully, was *very definitely* it!

At 8:30 the wind suddenly died down and visibility cleared almost magically. To his consternation, Waters now saw that over twenty enemy tanks were crawling like squat, evil, khaki-colored bugs to the west of his position. He was cut off from the rear! Five minutes later the number had risen to thirty-nine. And there seemed no end to the bastards. When he had counted over eighty enemy vehicles, he gave up counting. It was pretty obvious what had happened to the forward positions under the weight of such a massive German attack. Grimly Waters bit his bottom lip and considered for a moment what he should do next.

Realizing that he was completely surrounded, which the 1st Armored's staff officers had predicted to Fredendall when the general had first picked the position, he decided to move his command post—a half-track and a jeep— up the hill to avoid detection. Then, the German Mark

IV's would probably be unable to climb the hill, although the Arabs, who knew the place like the backs of their greedy brown hands, were already well in evidence. Waters knew from his months in North Africa that they were prepared to betray their grandmothers for anything that looked like money. Once they discovered his position, they would speedily inform the Krauts in order to get the reward the Germans always gave them for Allied prisoners.

After making his move, he called up Hains for the last time. "Don't worry about us," he told his commander, "we'll be all right. You get on with the war."

Little did he realize it then, but that telephone call was going to be his last official act of World War II.

That had occurred at ten o'clock in the morning. Now, late in the afternoon, Waters and his staff officer plus the jeep driver and the other young PFC who drove the White half-track crouched in a draw on Djebel Lessouda and watched their green division being eaten up by Rommel's veterans of the 10th Panzer Division.

With a feeling akin to despair, Waters saw tank after tank of the American division being "brewed up"—as the British 8th Army veterans described the process—by the German Mark IV's, which outgunned and outfought the green Americans in virtually every case. Now he knew that his position was desperate. As soon as the Germans had dealt with the few remaining American tanks which so far had managed to evade them, they would send up infantry to deal with the "Amis" remaining on Djebel Lessouda.

Making a quick but reluctant decision which went against all he had ever been taught at the Point, he decided he would pull back his men as soon as it grew dark. His decision made, he quickly scribbled a note to his infantry battalion commander telling him of his intention, and gave the note to the jeep driver to deliver.

The young soldier seized his M-1 and, stooping low so that he could not be seen from below, disappeared into the dirty brown rocks. Waters glanced at his back and then at his watch. God, he hoped it would get dark soon this day!

An hour of tense waiting went by. Down below more and more German vehicles barreled westward as if nothing or nobody was ever going to stop them. Preoccupied as he was with his own command's fate, Waters wondered what was happening to the rest of the division. This was obviously not just a local action, but a really big operation, probably commanded by the master himself—Erwin Rommel. Gloomily he concluded that the div wasn't doing too well under such heavy and skillfully directed pressure.

And then abruptly he was shaken out of his reverie. The jeep driver was staggering toward them! Blood poured down the front of his dusty uniform. His rifle and helmet were gone.

Quickly Waters sprang to his feet. Followed by the others, he ran urgently toward the wildly swaying young soldier.

"Colonel," he gasped, his breath coming in short shallow bursts, "I got shot!"

Waters nodded hurriedly. That was all too obvious. The man had a gaping wound in his chest and was bleeding profusely.

Gently he and the other staff officer lowered the wounded man to the hard, dusty ground and made a litter for him out of Waters' own bedroll while all the time the badly wounded man apologized for not having been able to deliver the vital message. What made it worse was that he believed he had been shot mistakenly by a trigger-happy fellow American.

As best he could, Waters calmed the man, telling him it didn't matter—though in his heart he knew that his infantry was also doomed now. Then he gave him a shot of morphine and made him as comfortable as possible. And while the wounded man's breathing grew deeper and harsher under the influence of the drug and he finally stopped chattering, the remaining three men settled down gloomily among the rocks, each sunk in his own thoughts.

Toward evening the firing began to slacken off—at least it seemed to have moved further westward in the wake of the bulk of the German armor which had long since passed that way. Waters guessed that the Krauts wouldn't stop now until they reached the mountain area behind them which went under the name of—if he remembered rightly —the Kasserine Pass.[5] Now he began to look anxiously at the sky. It was beginning to grow a little gray, he thought, hoping he wasn't deluding himself into believing that a change was taking place. Perhaps the Germans wouldn't discover them before it grew dark. Once it was dark, they would have a chance of getting away. At the moment, they would not last five minutes on the perfectly flat countryside down below which offered absolutely no cover whatsoever.

Suddenly his staff officer impinged on his thoughts. "Down there, sir!" he said and pointed to the valley.

A small band of marauding Arabs was moving in their direction, looking for weapons, food and—naturally— prisoners. It was time to move. Leaving the wounded man where he was, he ordered the other enlisted man to drive the half-track to another wadi about a hundred yards away, at the same time giving his staff officer instructions to find another hiding place elsewhere so that if the Germans were led to their positions by the Arabs, they wouldn't capture both of them. Another tense half hour passed, with Waters resting his hand on his pistol, ready to fight to the end if necessary. But nothing happened. No Arabs, no Krauts—no nothing. It was getting perceptibly darker and crouched there in the scrub, Waters really began to believe that they might be lucky after all and get away without being spotted.

Then suddenly his tired mind began to race again. Down below small German patrols of perhaps half a dozen men each were starting to move through the scrub, their weapons at the ready, their eyes carefully searching the area. It was obvious what they were looking for. American stragglers like themselves.

"Damnation!" Waters cursed to himself. Then he remembered the tubes were still in the half-track's radio;

---

[5] The action at the djebels was a preliminary to the first major battle fought by U.S. Troops in the European theater: the Battle of the Kasserine Pass.

he didn't want the Germans to get that. Turning to the driver who crouched tensely next to him, he whispered urgently. "Get the tubes and hide 'em!"

"Yessir."

Obediently the private scurried away at a half crouch to do the job.

Time passed. There were more and more German infantry appearing in their white-peaked caps. Waters looked at his watch. The driver should have done the darned job by now. Where the hell was he keeping himself? Then he heard footsteps. Someone was coming up the wadi toward him. It was the driver.

Quickly he rose to his feet to show the man where he was hiding. "*Here,*" he began, and the words froze on his lips.

Facing him at less than ten yards' distance were seven Kraut soldiers in Afrika Korps caps, and a couple of ragged Arabs in dirty gowns. They were the guides who had obviously betrayed his position to the Germans.

The enemy was as startled as he was. A nervous young soldier fired instinctively. A burst of lead from his machine pistol cut the air inches away from Waters' head. Quickly Waters raised his hands. *He was a prisoner of war!*

That had been two years ago. On that first day of his captivity the German patrol had marched him about half a mile to a mobile command post, where a group of exuberant young German officers were listening to dance music on the radio of a captured U.S. half-track. They were in tremendous spirits and talked about the "Battle of Tunisia" as already won. "Tomorrow," they boasted, "we will win the war."

Waters was too depressed to answer. "What about my driver?" he countered. The man was dead, he was told. The Arabs had stripped him of his clothing. Grimly Waters accepted the news, wondering to himself if the damned Arabs hadn't murdered the poor guy for his clothing and equipment.

Shortly thereafter he had been placed in a motorcycle sidecar, with a guard on the back, and had been driven

to the rear to a POW cage, a strip of desert, wired off
and covered by guards carrying grease guns. From there
he had been shipped to Sfax, Sousse and Tunis, where he
had crossed the Mediterranean for Italy. After the surrender of that country he had been transferred to Szubin
in Poland.

As the weeks became months and the months became
years, he grew to know that the German prison-of-war
camp could best be measured in degrees of starvation.
Right at the bottom of the starvation list were the lousy,
filthy, ragged Russians whose treatment was barbaric.
Then came the Italians and the French, who were tolerated
as ineffectual. At the top of the ladder came the British
and Americans. But even these "elite" prisoners were
treated little better than animals.

At 6:30 A.M. they were routed out of their huts to
stand at the appell roll-call formation for anything up
to ninety minutes before they received—thanks to the
Geneva Convention—"breakfast." A cup of acorn coffee
or flax tea, plus a two-inch slab of black bread spread
with *sirop,* treacle made from sugar beet.

At noon—again thanks to the Geneva Convention—
they received a piece of lard (in lieu of margarine), a
small bowl of potato soup, made of green or bad potatoes,
or even from nauseating sugar beet tops, which had to
last until supper, which was the noonday meal warmed
up with, on special occasions, such as the Fuehrer's birthday, a handful of cold boiled potatoes thrown in.

Sunday was the big day. On Sunday "meat" was served
—several grams of rank horse meat which was usually so
bad that everyone save the most hungry threw it away
on the spot. A few of the more ravenous cooked it over
a wood fire to burn out the taste and then gulped it down
quickly (and with their eyes closed so that they did not
see the maggots) with the aid of a glass of water.

The high spot of the month was the Red Cross parcel,
which according to the Geneva rules the kriegies were
supposed to receive once a week. They never did. And
even when they got it, some camp commandants could not
resist taking the pleasure out of this monthly treat. Some

of the more sadistic Germans would order that all cans should be opened at once so that they could not be hoarded "for an escape." The result was that the angry prisoner, often on the verge of tears, received his cans of spam, salmon and corned beef already opened. He would then have to eat the lot at once so that the food wouldn't spoil, with disastrous effect on his stomach weakened by months of starvation diet.

Complaints about food always received the same answer. "It's because of your terror bombers which are disrupting our centers of supply." And that was that.

Thus the two long years since 1943 had passed for the handsome young Regular Army colonel. He had become so accustomed to the misery, the starvation, the bravery of POW camp life that sometimes he almost forgot that there was anything else beyond that dreary square of barbed wire with its high wooden towers and machine guns.

But now he was on the outside again—even though still under guard. And he knew he had had enough; he wanted to see his wife and kids again. He wanted to get back into the war before it was too damned late; after all, he was a career officer and career officers made their reputations in times of war and not of peace.

Frustrated and angry, Colonel John Waters plodded on day after day[6] at the side of Pop Goode, moving ever further westward for an unknown destination and his own particular date with destiny. John Waters, husband of "Little B," favorite daughter of General George S. Patton, was getting ever nearer to the victorious Third Army commanded by his father-in-law!

---

[6] Eventually their condition forced the Germans to transport them into the interior of the *Reich* by rail.

Chapter 2

The opinionated General Fredendall did not long survive the Kasserine Pass debacle, the first major U.S. action and first major U.S. defeat in the Battle of the West. Eisenhower relieved him of his corps and sent him back home to be—as the British put it—"kicked upstairs." He was promoted to three-star general, given a hero's welcome and the command of the 2nd Training Army, where his "ability in training troops especially after his recent battle experience"[1] might be employed. Thereupon he was promptly forgotten; history has no time for failures.

He was replaced by a man who—according to a worried and publicity-conscious Eisenhower—was a "leading tank expert," though the "expert" had had nothing to do with tanks until recently for nearly 20 years. In fact, he was regarded by many regular officers as the Army's leading cavalry man, if only because he loved horses.

The "leading tank expert" had other names, however, which were not so complimentary. One of the best-hated men in the Regular Army, he had been known shortly before the war as the "Madman of Fort Clark".[2] Then with the coming of the war he had been baptized the "Green Hornet" on account of his self-designed uniform with its bright green color and strange futuristic helmet which was oddly similar to those worn twenty years later by the spacemen. He was called many other names too, but they cannot be used in polite circles. The name that finally stuck to him, however, for the rest of his short life would characterize him aptly enough as a man who

---

[1] Note in the diary of Captain Butcher U.S.N., Eisenhower's long-time aide and confidant.

[2] So-called in Washington because of his peculiar training habits, and his pathological insistence on spit and polish.

loved war and everything that went with it; the blood, the tension, the power and—above all—the glory. It was simply "Old Blood and Guts." General George S. Patton Jr. had arrived on the scene!

General Patton was for many, especially the great U.S. public the epitome of the American frontier tradition. His nickname itself was sufficient to indicate the tough, rough, brawling, masculine figure he was. He was violent and vulgar, concerned with getting the right snarl on the thin lips of what he called his "war face" and with the impact of his image as a "pistol-packing fightin' general."[3] When he got up to address his men, he pulled no punches and his language was liberally salted with "goddams," "s.o.b.'s" and worse. Speaking to a new division about to go into the line for the first time, he told them:

> If any instructor back home told you to hit the dirt when enemy rifle or machine fire started, he was asking you to come over here and commit suicide. The German is no fool. He will shoot over your heads at a given spot, you'll dive to the ground, he's got his mortars zeroed in and you'll end up so chewed apart, even the buzzards wouldn't touch you. The thing to do is to keep running forward and to keep firing. The Hun won't expect it and he'll be more scared than you are. The way most new soldiers use their rifles, they are no more use than a pecker is to the Pope.[4]

Another new division was told:

> Battle is far less frightening than those who have never been in it are apt to think. All this bull about thinking of your mother and your sweetheart and your wives (who should also be your sweethearts) is emphasized by [what] writers who have never heard a hostile shot or missed a meal think they are. Battle is the most magnificent competition in which a human being can indulge. It brings out

---

[3] He was always concerned that people should know that his pistols were ivory, *not* pearl-handled. As he once told his nephew Fred Ayer: "Goddam my guns are ivory-handled. Nobody but a pimp for a cheap New Orleans whorehouse would carry one with a pearl grip!"

[4] When reminded later that his eloquence had carried him away again, he groaned and said: "Oh, my God, now I guess I'll have to write a letter of apology to the Vatican!"

all that is best; it removes all that is base. All men are
afraid in battle. The coward is the one who lets his fear
overcome his sense of duty. Duty is the essence of man-
hood. Americans pride themselves on being he-men and
they *are* he-men.

As he once summed up his whole attitude to his nephew
Fred Ayer, it was simply: "The man who won't fuck, won't
fight!"

Yet there was something arrogant, aristocratic and very
definitely un-American about George S. Patton. The tall
distinguished-looking soldier with the belligerent face, hard
eyes and close-cropped hair had been born independently
wealthy and had married into the family of a Bostonian
textile tycoon who was so grand that even his own children
called him "Sir Frederick." As the lowest man on the
totem pole the young shavetail second lieutenant of cavalry
at the start of his military career, and his wife, had always
dressed for dinner, even in the tight confines of the couple
of bare rooms in the fort to which they were assigned. The
sight of the Pattons in their evening dress earned for them
straightaway the malicious, envious title of the "Duke and
Duchess."

After World War I, young Major Patton could always
afford the finest accommodation in the nearest town, mo-
toring back and forth to duty in the latest and most expensive automobile available. He ran a string of polo
ponies at a time during the Depression when the average
Army officer of the same rank was lucky to have a single
ancient steed at his disposal; and the same polo ponies invariably aroused the ire of much less wealthy commanders
who frequently ordered Patton to take the ponies off the
post, which he did, billeting them at the nearest livery
stable at his own expense. In short, the Pattons' private
life was aristocratic and upper class, a black-tie affair in
the best society; his professional life was the contrived,
rather shabby middle-class one of the Army.

Patton had an aristocratic way with the men who served
under him too. There was no easy, typically American,
democratic informality about him. One had to be at least
an army commander to call him "George," while the di-

minutive "Georgie" was reserved for a few select superiors such as Bradley and Eisenhower.

This was the general who in Sicily in 1943 let his autocratic temper carry him away to the extent that he forgot himself completely and was involved in the famous face-slapping incident. Major Ettner, who was there, describes the incident graphically in the report he was ordered to prepare on the matter for the Corps Surgeon:

On Monday afternoon August 10, 1943, at approximately 1330, General Patton entered the Receiving Ward of the 93rd Evacuation Hospital and started interviewing and visiting the patients who were there. There were some 10 or 15 casualties in the tent at the time. The first five or six that he talked to were battle casualties. He asked each what his trouble was, commended them for their excellent fighting; told them they were doing a fine job, and wished them a speedy recovery. He came to one patient, who, on inquiry, stated that he was sick with high fever. The general dismissed him without comment. The next patient was sitting huddled up and shivering. When asked what his trouble was, the man replied, "It's my nerves," and began to sob. The General then screamed at him. "What did you say?" He replied, "It's my nerves, I can't bear the shelling any more." He was still sobbing.

The General then yelled at him, "Your nerves, Hell, you are just a Goddam coward, you yellow son of a bitch!" He then slapped the man and said, "Shut up that Goddamned crying. I won't have these brave men here who have been shot seeing a yellow bastard sitting here crying!" He then struck at the man again, knocking his helmet liner off and into the next tent. He then turned to the Receiving Officer and yelled, "Don't you admit this yellow bastard, there's nothing the matter with him. I won't have the hospitals cluttered up with these sons of bitches who haven't got the guts to fight!"

He turned to the man again, who was managing to "sit to attention" though shaking all over and said, "You're going back to the front lines and you may get shot and killed, but you're going to fight. If you don't, I'll stand you up against the wall and have a firing squad kill you on purpose. In fact," he said, reaching for his pistol, "I ought to shoot you myself, you Goddamned whimpering coward." As he went out of the ward he was still yelling back at the

Receiving Officer to send that yellow son of a bitch to the
front lines . . .

Thus Patton at his most autocratic.

His approach to battle was equally autocratic and un-
American, in the sense that Americans are supposed to
hate war. Patton didn't; he loved it and he was frank about
his love affair with violent death. Once, riding down a
French road in the summer of 1944, he and his aid Colonel
Codman came upon a scene of terrible destruction. An
unprotected German column had been caught on the road
by Allied fighter bombers and had been slaughtered.
American bulldozers had swept a path clear through the
frightful carnage, thrusting the reeking, bloody mess of
blackened German corpses, smashed half-tracks and
burned-out trucks to one side. Patton, seeing the mess,
ordered his car stopped and as Codman describes it:

> Encompassing with a sweep of his arm the rubbled farms
> and bordering fields scarred with grass fires, smoldering
> ruins, and the swollen carcasses of stiff-legged cattle, the
> General half turned in his seat. "Just look at that, Codman,"
> he shouted. "Could anything be more magnificent?" As we
> passed a clump of bushes, one of our concealed batteries let
> go with a shattering salvo. The General cupped both
> hands. I leaned forward to catch his words. "Compared to
> war, all other forms of human endeavor shrink to insig-
> nificance!" His voice shook with emotion. *"God, how I
> love it!"*

And it is not insignificant that his favorite military motto
was borrowed from Europe's greatest military autocrat,
Frederick the Great: *"L'audace, l'audace, toujours l'audace."*

His boss, Omar Bradley, a man of humble origins, un-
ostentatious conduct and simple middle-class habits saw
through him and recognized him for what he was. Once, in
irritation, he wrote:

> Canny a showman though George was, he failed to grasp
> the pyschology of the combat soldier . . . He traveled in
> an entourage of command cars followed by a string of
> nattily uniformed staff officers. His own vehicle was gaily
> decked with oversize stars and the insignia of his com-
> mand. *These exhibitions did not awe the troops as perhaps
> Patton believed. Instead they offended them as they trudged*

through the clouds of dust left in the wake of that procession [author's italics].

After the face-slapping incident in Sicily and the resultant scandal (which, although Eisenhower tried to hush it up, nearly cost Patton his commission, and several others subsequently) Old Blood and Guts was forced to eat humble pie for many months. Everywhere he went he was regarded as bad news. No one wanted to have anything to do with him. Forced to go to hospital in London to have a sore on his lip treated, he quipped: "After all the ass-kissing I have to do here, no wonder I have a sore lip!"

The Normandy Invasion came and went without George S. Patton. It was two months after D Day before his Third Army was allowed to swing into action, taking part in what was basically a side show—the Brittany Campaign. As Captain Harry Butcher, Eisenhower's aide wrote contemptuously, perhaps reflecting his boss's own attitude: "Patton had taken command yesterday and it was obvious that he had plunged ahead against little or no resistance."

But Patton had a canny eye for publicity and he always gave a fine dramatic performance for the correspondents attached to his headquarters so that he was invariably excellent copy. Reading through the yellowed pages of the newspapers of that period, there seems hardly an issue without mention of General Patton on the front page under banner headlines. He overshadowed the other Army commanders completely—so much so that Butcher, who was responsible for SHAEF publicity, complained:

If the correspondents with the Third Army don't mention Patton, apparently the headline writers at home insert his name. In any event, Patton is getting great publicity and is overshadowing Hodges of the U.S. 1st Army. I have "made a signal" to the PRO of First Army suggesting that the correspondents there be encouraged to write of that army as Hodges's. This may balance the credit. But it takes a lot of color in any man to balance Patton.

As the European campaign progressed, Patton's fame steadily increased. He came out of the Battle of the Bulge as the "liberator of Bastogne," (the only successful defense of the whole sorry Ardennes battle), the sole Allied senior commander whose reputation was unimpaired. His Third Army fought on stolidly through the miserable winter of 1944/45, and although he did not achieve the brilliant breakthrough to the Rhine which Patton always sought, he suffered none of the failures which virtually every other Allied commander did. Patton had found a way to overcome the "wraps" which he complained to his intimates the high command—Eisenhower and Montgomery, in his opinion—had placed upon him.[5] It was what he called his "rock soup" method of getting a campaign started without official permission.

"A tramp," he explained to his staff one day, "once went to a house and asked for some boiling water to make a rock soup. The lady was interested and gave him the water in which he placed two polished white stones. He then asked if he might have some potatoes and carrots to flavor it a little and finally ended up with some meat."

"In other words," he spelled out the practical meaning of the parable, "in order to attack we'll have to pretend to reconnoiter, then reinforce the reconnaissance and finally put on the attack."

The method had paid off in Lorraine, in the Eifel and later in the Rhineland so that by the spring of 1945 Patton was regaining his old aristocratic form. Back home his name was a household word, daily fare for an admiring public, who knew little of Hodges, Simpson or Devers. At the front his men might have hated his guts and his insistence on the daily shave and necktie,[6] but they were aggressive and consistently victorious. At his headquarters he was surrounded by mediocre admiring officers, such as Colonel Codman, who could write:

> He [Patton] has contributed to the science of warfare professional proficiency of the highest modern order. More significantly, however, and it is this that sets him apart, he brings to the art of command in this day and age the norms and antique virtues of the classic warrior . . . In the

---

[5] Once he complained to Bradley: "Goddamit Brad, why the hell won't SHAEF leave us alone! I'd rather fight the Hun than Ike and Monty all the time!"

[6] Patton's Third Army was kept trim by an elaborate system of fines for infringements of his dress regulations.

time of Roger the Norman or in ancient Rome, General Patton would have felt completely at home.

Very fulsome praise, indeed, and not isolated. For instance, his chief of staff, one-eyed General Gay, could speak of him as the "bravest man I know." For Patton there was no fiery-tempered Bedell Smith of Eisenhower's HQ, who could state bluntly that "somebody around here has to be a son-of-a-bitch!" There were none of "Monty's young men," who although they were only lowly captains and majors were freely allowed to criticize the "master's" plans.[7] As the American novelist John Marquand wrote somewhat cynically after spending a day at Patton's HQ and taking a dinner there:

It was a very good dinner too, faintly reminiscent of grownups and children's tables at a Thanksgiving party. The Generals were the grownups, the staff officers the children.

That spring, highly successful, assured of public admiration, surrounded by his obedient, hero-worshiping "children," General George S. Patton Jr. was again his old arrogant, aristocratic self. Freed from any restraint, commanding 600,000 men, the largest single army that the United States had ever fielded, Patton once again felt himself above the dictates of such ordinary mortals as Eisenhower and Bradley, both of whom he despised for what he considered their pedestrian lack of military ability.[8]

That spring, the man who took up his new command in Algiers on Sunday, March 7, 1943 with tears in his eyes because of the bad news he had just received,[9] was about

---

[7] It is clear from the memoirs of Montgomery's generals, such as Sir Francis De Guingand and Sir Brian Horrocks, who owed everything to the Field Marshal, that they were well aware of his shortcomings. Of the many memoirs written about Patton there is not one which swerves from the path of completely uncritical admiration.

[8] In front of his staff Patton consistently sniped against 'Ike', whom he considered (because of his stern support of Montgomery) the 'best general the British have' and 'a good future president, but no soldier.'

[9] Butcher, in his Three Years with Eisenhower, describes the scene as follows: "Ike and Patton . . . conferred standing up for half an hour at the airfield. Patton, who normally hates the Hun—as

to commit what he was to depict with characteristic lack of modesty as his "only mistake of the European campaign."

Ike says, like the devil hates holy water—and who now is all the more embittered because his son-in-law, Johnnie Waters, is reported missing in action—damned the Germans so violently and emotionally that tears came to his eyes three times during the short conference."

Chapter 3

The meal so far had been outstanding. Patton was a little red in the face from the good food and drink, and although he was not a great or fussy eater, he was looking forward to the next course—a roast. Around the great table, the top brass—Bradley, Simpson, Hodges, Gerow and the French general who had presented them with the Legion of Honor that morning, General Juin—chatted animatedly with one another, their tongues loosened by the wine and whiskey. Silent for once, Patton wondered what would happen if a bomb suddenly dropped on the illustrious group. There'd be a lot of quick promotions in the United States Army, he concluded a little cynically and reached once more for his glass. Tonight he would indulge himself a little more than his usual two whiskies and water.

Suddenly he was shaken out of his reverie. A staff officer slipped quietly into the room, came directly to his seat and whispered *sotto voce,* "For you, sir."

It was a wire.

Swiftly Patton slipped on his glasses, (in which he was never photographed; he felt they marred the impression made by his "war face") and read the few lines. With a grunt he pushed back his chair and while the others watched him curiously, stalked out of the room, soon to be followed by Bradley, to whom he passed the message.

It was from General Gay, his one-eyed chief of staff. It informed Patton that General Matt Eddy's men, in particular the 2d Cavalry, had secured a bridge intact across the Moselle River. Eddy had asked Gay what he should do and, off his own bat, Gay had told him to exploit his bridgehead and form a firm base for further attack.

Patton looked at Bradley when they were alone. "Well?" he asked.

Bradley did not hesitate. "Go ahead, Georgie," he said.

Patton needed no urging. Immediately he placed a call to General Gay. It came through within a matter of minutes. Presumably the staff officer had been waiting by the telephone for the call. Quickly Patton told Gay to go ahead with the attack and that he, Patton, had been given the SHAEF general reserve division—the 80th Division—to back up the attack.

Patton was all smiles when he returned to the great room of the *château* which housed Bradley's headquarters. Before he sat down, he stopped by the chair of General Juin. The French general had been needling him a little previously about allowing Hodges to steal a march on him by capturing the Remagen Bridge, the first intact one across the Rhine. Now Patton bent over, the light capturing the sheen of his close-cropped silver hair. *"Monsieur le General,"* he said softly, "when you get to Paris, don't fail to read your favorite newspaper."

The French officer looked up puzzled at Patton's face, and the latter allowed himself a slight smile of triumph. "Because within a day or two you will see who is stealing a march on whom."

Patton had just ordered Gay to not only exploit the captured bridge, but also—against orders—to launch the prearranged Palatinate Campaign which would take the Third Army up to the city of Koblenz and the River Rhine, the last major water barrier.[1]

---

[1] Two hours later Eddy telephoned Gay and told him they hadn't captured a bridge after all. When the first 2d Cav tank had begun to cross it, the Germans had blown it and the tank sky high. Gay responded in a typical Patton manner. He told Eddy he wanted a bridge by the morning, adding, "Matt, if you don't do it, I shall be a private!" When Patton returned, he ordered all lines to higher authority cut until Eddy managed to secure another bridge across the Moselle and the campaign could proceed. As the Australian historian Chester Wilmot truly remarked: "He [Patton] had to finagle to accomplish a remarkable feat" [the Palatinate Campaign].

One day prior to that decision, some ninety miles away in the interior of the Reich, a long decrepit troop train pulled in at the great German training ground of Hammelburg high in the Spessart Hills. On that cold, gloomy Thursday of March 8, 1945, the surviving 430 kriegies of the 1,400 who had left Szubin, Poland the month before finally reached their destination.

Laden with gray Wehrmacht blankets rolled in a bandolier around their bodies, homemade cooking stoves which would burn anything including dried horse manure, rucksacks made out of old sugar sacks, they dropped out of the flat carts, tired, stiff, hungry and dirty, and took a first look at their new home.

Oflag VII, the officers' prisoner-of-war camp, was not a very inspiring sight on that gray March day. It lay on the top of the saucer-shaped plateau of a large hill overlooking the little wine town of Hammelburg, where they had made wine since the time of Charlemagne, and out to the great windy artillery and rifle ranges, where German troops had trained for over fifty years.

The camp itself was made up of two compounds. The larger of the two housed nearly 5,000 Yugoslav officers (they preferred to call themselves Serbs) who had been captured in 1941. They were shabby yet proud men, in spite of the fact they felt they had been abandoned by the Allies in favor of the new Communist leader of their country, Tito.[2] Under the leadership of the elderly generals of the Yugoslav General Staff (the whole staff was present at Hammelburg), the great majority of the dark-faced, hawk-nosed officers tried to fight back the increasing influence of the few Communist officers and the Russians in their midst.[3]

---

[2] Tito began to be recognized as the main resistance leader around 1943, and thereafter received most of the Allied supplies dropped in Yugoslavia.

[3] The most prominent Russian POW had been Captain Stalin, son of the Russian dictator. A morose, ill-mannered officer, he continually quarreled with his fellow POW's. Later, after a fist fight with a British POW, he reportedly crossed to the wire and after being warned by a guard to get away, was shot down and killed from one of the towers.

The smaller compound, a collection of low two-story huts, made of stone and wood, housed the American officer prisoners. Now there were some 1,400 of them quartered in the former German Army stables, which were surrounded by eight-foot-high wire fences and guarded by some ten or twelve wooden-legged towers, each containing a German guard armed with a machine gun.

Goode, still clutching his precious bagpipes which he was still determined to learn to play and which contained a few secret papers and—more important—vital radio parts from the Szubin Camp receiver, stared morosely at the camp and its occupants, while John Waters stood by his side in glum silence. Neither the camp nor the American prisoners impressed the middle-aged colonel. To his eyes the elderly guards with their long French rifles and those crouched in the towers over their Belgian machine guns, looked jumpy and nervous, and Goode estimated that it wouldn't take too much provocation for them to use their itchy trigger fingers.[4]

As for the kriegies, they looked scruffy, ragged and unkempt to Goode's trained Regular Army eye, with most of the younger men sporting dark sloppy growths of beard which contrasted oddly with their shaved heads. Goode stared at them as they stood there in the cold wind which always blew across the bleak plateau, their hands burrowed deeply in their combat jacket pockets, their shoulders hunched, feet shuffling to keep warm as they gazed at the new arrivals with lackluster eyes and felt one of his sudden angers begin to grow within him.

He knew full well that the miserable diet of prison-camp food could do to a man's morale if he were limited to it month in, month out. But he knew too that discipline and a sense of purpose could overcome famine, boredom and

---

[4]Prior to Goode's arrival several Serbian officers were shot dead by nervous guards although they had not committed any crime. As a result, one of the camp's officers was arrested in 1948 as a war criminal and sent to Yugoslavia, where he was executed. Soon it would be the turn of U.S. officers to be shot without provocation.

despair if they were correctly applied. These men were obviously ill-disciplined. As weary and emotionally worn-out as he was, he promised himself that if he got a chance to take over, he would change a lot of things at Hammelburg Prisoner of War Camp—and damned quick at that!

He was abruptly jerked out of his reverie. The goons had started their usual Teutonic bellowing: *"Los . . . los, Mensch . . . mach schnell!"* (Pop Goode wondered sometimes whether he would ever be able to forget the same old raucous commands, even when the war was over and he was a free man again.) Slowly the ragged column began to form. Officiously the NCO's made the Americans get into line, harassing them all the while. More orders were rapped out and the prisoners turned to the right.

Goode and Waters placed themselves at the head of the column next to old Lieutenant Colonel Huff, a tough former enlisted man, who stood as straight as a ramrod in spite of his burden. Together the three of them searched the area for the cause of the harassment. As Regular Army officers themselves ("Old Heads" the younger officers called them, half in scorn, half in admiration), they knew that NCO's only moved that smartly when superior brass was within range. Then they spotted the cause of the sudden alacrity. A tall, slim officer was standing watching the column from the doorway of the big stone building to their left. He wore the bay leaves and red stripe of a general. Goode gave Waters a furtive nudge "The commandant," he whispered. Waters gave him a significant look and nodded his agreement. This was going to be their new boss. But now they had not time to study the German general further. The column was ready to move off.

Goode straightened up. Suddenly he forgot his burden. He was going to show the Krauts and the watching kriegies! He rapped out a command with the authority of decades of Army service behind it. The ragged column came to attention. Then in perfect formation the newcomers marched through the gate and down Hermann Goering Strasse, with Pop Goode, head held high, proudly stepping

out at their head.[5] Behind them the gate of Hammelburg
Lager clanged closed with a note of hollow finality.

Tall, straight-backed General von Goeckel watched the
new arrivals depart and then he heaved a sigh. *Mehr
Amerikaner!* And *natürlich,* more problems.

Since he had taken over the camp in August 1944, he
had found the handful of Americans who had first started
to come in that October more of a problem than the many
thousand Serbian officers under his command. They were
even more of a discipline problem than the handful of
Russians, who because they were not protected by the
Geneva Convention, were half starved and consequently
always in trouble on account of their light-fingered habits.
A regular German Army officer since 1908, von Goeckel,
who had been badly wounded in the lung in World War I
and had consequently always held staff jobs since then, did
not really understand *"Meine Amis,"* as he called his
American prisoners to his own staff.

Some of them were naturally of the same type he had
known in the German Army: career officers, whom he
respected because of their bearing, conduct and character. But these were usually the older and senior men.
Most of the younger men were, in his opinion, "silly high
school kids, who would never have been promoted to
officer rank in the German Army." They were "often un-
believably infantile" and showed no respect for either their
own senior officers or the German ones, even Captain
Fuchs, a middle-aged gentleman, who spoke English and
seemed generally well accepted by most of the Americans.

Goeckel sighed again and, screwing up his neck in that
peculiar manner of those who suffer from lung complaints,
fought for breath. Even twenty-odd years after being
wounded, he still found it difficult to breathe correctly
with his one remaining lung.

Hoffentlich this new transport of Americans wouldn't
be as bad as the last lot who had arrived soon after the
Battle of the Bulge. They had been a pathetic group of lost

[5]Many of the senior officers who watched that entrance testify to
the thrill of pride it gave them to see Goode's men march in
like that.

young men, who had—or so it seemed to him—relinquished all respect for themselves and the Army to which they had once belonged. Some of them had lain all day long in their bunks, sunk in dejected apathy. Others had gone to pieces completely, neither washing nor shaving for days on end, even needing to be forced by their comrades to go outside to the latrine to relieve themselves. It wasn't at all what he had expected from these representatives of the New World, or—as his middle-aged militia called the United States in their more cynical moments—"the land of the unlimited possibilities."

"Na ja," he murmured to himself and temporarily dismissed the unpleasant thought of the problems the new Americans might occasion him. Soon his tall, pretty wife, who had fled from the advancing Russians and was now living with him in a cell-like room in the officers' quarters together with several relatives and the sharp-tongued wife of Major Hoppe, the commander of the next-door Army training camp, would be bringing him his midday meal. It wouldn't be anything to look forward to—*Erbsen-Suppe,* with a hunk of *ersatz* sausage in it, if he were lucky. But it was better than nothing and he didn't like to keep his wife waiting. He'd better get across to the theater and address the new arrivals. He wondered how they would take the fact that they were almost completely unexpected (Berlin had failed again) and that there were very few spare supplies available for them. Perhaps the Serbs would help out again by donating some of their own Red Cross supplies from the huge store they had accumulated over the years? Perhaps they would. He would see . . .

Pop Goode gave himself a few days to recover from the privations of the long trip to Hammelburg, then he sprang into action, determined to get the camp into shape. His first task was to relieve Colonel Charles Cavender, the camp's senior American officer until then.

Cavender, the former commander of the 423rd Infantry Regiment and a former World War I doughboy, had surrendered his regiment in the Snow Eifel after two days of combat at the start of the Battle of the Bulge and, because of this action, was resented by the more senior American prisoners and disobeyed by the younger ones.[6] Cavender was only too eager to get rid of the unrewarding post and passed it over to Goode with alacrity.

Goode, aided by the modest yet highly competent Colonel Waters and his "inspector general," rough, tough old Colonel Huff, set about reorganizing the Oflag. His first problem was the morale of the majority of the men under his control.

Most of them had been captured during the Battle of the Bulge and most of them had never quite recovered from the shock of the first few shameful days of that sneak attack when many of the raw green outfits guarding the "ghost front"[7] had broken, run and finally surrendered in the thousands.

Some had stayed and fought to the last or until they could fight no more. Major Don Boyer, of the 7th Armored Division, was such a man who had fought with his armored infantrymen until they had been abandoned by their own command as the rear at the Battle of St.-Vith to be overrun by German tanks. Another such man was big burly Colonel Joe Matthews, former executive officer of the 422nd Infantry Regiment, who had cussed the Germans ever since he had been captured and refused to let his spirit be broken.

Another was twenty-one-year-old Lieutenant John H. Hemingway, son of the famous writer. While his father had enjoyed a "great old time" in the Paris Ritz with his "Hemingstein Bearded Junior Commandos,"[8] his son had parachuted into southern France with an OSS outfit. His job had been to train the Maquis in the Montpellier area in infiltrating enemy positions.

---

[6] General von Goeckel thought Cavender "a pleasant officer who had, however, no control over his men."

[7] "Ghost front" because nothing was supposed ever to happen there. That December the Ardennes was regarded basically as a training ground for new divisions and a rest area for those which had been badly battered on other sectors of the front.

[8] A group of men from the 4th Infantry Division with whom Hemingway, although officially a war correspondent, had served on a combat basis in France and Germany.

Late in October he had been making a daytime reconnaissance along the valley of the River Rhône with a Captain Justin Green and one of the French partisans when he heard digging from within a grove of trees. The captain crawled forward to investigate. It was a fatal mistake. The Germans opened up with rifles and grenades. Green was wounded in the foot, Hemingway in the right arm and shoulder by grenade fragments and six rounds from a high-velocity carbine. The Frenchman was killed.

Taken prisoner by the members of an elite German alpine unit, they escaped being shot as spies by the lucky chance that the German officer in charge had been skiing in Brums in 1925 and had met the Hemingways including young John as a two-year-old toddler. The German rapidly ended the interrogation and sent the two men off to a regular POW camp and from there to Hammelburg, where young Hemingway, recovered from his wounds, was as defiant and cocky as his father to his captors.

But the great majority of the men came from the ill-fated 106th Infantry Division, the greenest division on any Allied front of the war that December when the Battle of the Bulge had started. Panicked by the sudden attack on a front which they had been told was used solely for training, trapped on all sides by the Germans, they had surrendered without putting up too much of a fight—nearly 10,000 of them. It was the second biggest surrender of U.S. troops since the Civil War, and the official U.S. history of the war has called it the "Most serious reverse suffered by U.S. arms" during the European campaign.

Marched to the rear in the third week of December, 1944, they had been repeatedly bombed by their own aircraft in a score of small towns and villages behind the German front so that it appeared to some of them that their own Army was paying them back for their shameful surrender. Forced into icy railroad wagons, they had suffered frostbitten toes and fingers in the crowded slow trains, which proceeded at a snail's pace in the coldest winter Europe had experienced in thirty years. Their discipline broke in several instances. At each station at which they halted, they begged pathetically for food and water and wept openly when the guards, enraged by Allied bombing raids on German cities, knocked the helmets filled with water, from their frozen fingers. Before the shocked eyes of haggard German *Hausfrauen,* they relieved themselves by the hundred wherever the train stopped and, when the guards would not allow them out any more as a result, they used the floors of the flat cars as a latrine. As Andrew Rooney, a *Stars and Stripes* reporter wrote at the time:

> After the battle men tore off their roaring Golden Lion badge (the divisional sign) . . . and conscientious battle casualties among them wept at the thought they had let the Army down.

After two months at Hammelburg, they had still built up no internal kriegie organization, as was customary at most POW camps. Unlike the Serbs, who had their own hobby shops, where they made their own furniture, or their theater, whose productions were honored by the presence of General von Goeckel, the Americans had no form of organization whatsoever, save for the Sunday mass held by Father Cavanaugh. A fine Catholic priest in his late 30's, he had rallied his comrades of the 106th often enough during the journey to the camp when they had been bombed and ill-treated, and he now tried to hold them together in the only way he knew how—through God.

There were no combines to collect, cook and distribute food and organize the daily routine of each room; no tunnels and escape committees; no camp universities with their discussion groups and foreign language classes. There was nothing save a monomaniacal concentration on the occasional Red Cross parcel and the starvation diet, which included such camp specialities as "Green Hornet" soup[9]

---

[9]"Green Hornet" soup was made of beet tops and horse meat. It got its name because when it was served, its surface was invariably covered with maggots stained green from the beets. Among the *kriegies* long and heated discussions were carried on as to whether they should remove the maggots or eat them. Colonel Joe Matthews, a former agricultural chemist, was of the opinion that *they should be eaten as a valuable source of protein.* Few *kriegies,* needless to say, agreed with him.

twice a day and the daily eight ounces of bread, made up of one third grain, one third chestnuts, and one third sawdust!

Goode lammed into the dispirited 106th men without mercy. First, beards were to come off. Then uniforms were ordered pressed (by lining the inner side of the crease with soap and sleeping on the uniform) and shoes shined or at least cleaned—with vaseline where no polish was available. The barracks were organized into combines with each officer taking his turn cleaning and carrying. Discipline became strict and Goode ordered that senior American as well as German officers should be saluted and spoken to respectfully.

Goeckel began to respect the new American colonel. He saw that the latter was a "tough person and a wild soldier" who wasn't "afraid of tearing into a sloppy or ill-disciplined fellow American even in my presence." And Goeckel realized that although Goode was feared by many, he was also respected, perhaps even liked by a few.[10]

He started to make concessions. As far as it lay in his power, he tried to improve the food. Red Cross parcels were handed out with the prisoners jostling each other in their eagerness to get them after the goons had carried out their routine search of the parcels' contents. Appells were canceled when the weather was bad and better medical care was given to those who were sick, though the doctors had only a few drugs and paper bandages at their disposal to look after the many score who went sick each week with diphtheria and dysentery. Twice Goeckel took Goode for a ride in his car down to the town of Hammelburg to have a look at the little place, but Goode was not impressed by the favor. Whenever one of his men was shot

---

[10]Camp rumor had it that Goode had always been on "somebody's shit-list" throughout his Army career and that this had been the cause of his slow promotion. Besides, he always expressed his opinions without hesitation or concession to rank. Rumor also had it that he had been captured leading an attack on a Normandy village because he had felt his 29th Infantry outfit shouldn't attack, but if they were ordered to do so (as they were), then he would go along with them.

at by a guard because he was too slow getting inside when Allied planes flew over the camp, or whenever they were fired upon crawling under the wire that separated them from the Serbian camp, he rushed immediately to Goeckel's office to protest in most heated and energetic manner.

Morale began to improve. The bearing of the younger officers changed noticeably. They started to take pride in themselves again. With the aid of the secret camp radio, they began to follow the course of the war again and repeatedly Goode assured them that they *must* hold on; they wouldn't be prisoners much longer. Even though the food ration was cut again a few days after Goode had gained concessions from Goeckel, American ingenuity made the best of it, even creating pies out of breadcrumbs, marmalade made of German turnip *sirop,* baking powder composed—of all things—of tooth powder, the baking done with shaving cream for grease! In spite of the weekly toll of deaths—some fifteen to twenty each week—the lack of food, the bitter cold on the exposed saucer-shaped plateau, Hammelburg Lager under Goode's command slowly began to resemble a military establishment, and evenings when "Pop" fell dog-tired into his bed, Waters would reassure him that in spite of everything he was doing a "damned good job."

Thus March began to draw to a close. Now when the lights were doused of an evening, the prisoners fell asleep full of new confidence in themselves and their future. But long after they were asleep, General von Goeckel lay sleepless in his cell-like room, fighting for breath yet trying not to wake his wife who lay at his side; she had suffered enough in these last few months. The tall German general knew by now that the war was lost, yet he knew too that he must do his duty to the end, whatever the outcome. Often in those long March nights he would turn and look at his wife's pretty face and wonder what would become of her when *it* happened. Soon they would come. Twice he had requested his headquarters in Nuremberg for permission to evacuate the camp, but his requests had been refused. In other words, higher headquarters expected him to de-

fend the camp with his three hundred middle-aged military
rejects armed with their antiquated captured French and
Belgian weapons, and whatever regular troops Major
Hoppe could place at his disposal. To placate headquarters
and to satisfy his honor as a soldier, he had ordered three
positions to be built, which would be manned if and when
the camp was attacked. But he knew with hopeless finality
that he hadn't a chance when they came—as they surely
would. In that final week of March the elderly general lay
awake night after night listening to the sound of the artillery barrage, faint but definitely there and drawing closer
and closer. General George S. Patton's Third Army was
on its way!

Chapter 4

While outside the heavies rumbled on, adding to the persistent background music of war, Patton faced pudgy, bespectacled General Eddy, commander of XII Corps, and snapped, "We've got to get a bridgehead at once! Every day we save means saving hundreds of American lives!" Eddy frowned and stared at Patton's immaculate uniform with the gleaming brasses, his fancy London britches, and lacquered helmet with its outside stars. Uneasily, he felt his blood pressure begin to mount again; it was always the same when he had to deal with Georgie Patton. "But, General," he protested, "I'm not ready yet." As he uttered the words, he remembered it was only six weeks ago that he had made a similar protest to Patton. "Goddamit, General, you never give me time to get ready!" he had exploded then. "The trouble with you is that you have no appreciation of the time and space factor in this war." "Is that so?" Old Blood and Guts had replied calmly. "If I had any appreciation of it, we'd still be sitting on the Seine."

This time, Patton did not even bother to reply. "What are you waiting for?" he cried instead. "We can take the river at the run."

The river to be taken "at the run" was Europe's major water barrier—the Rhine, which the Third Army had just reached that March day. Now Patton wanted his men across before Field Marshal Montgomery could launch his own spectacular crossing of the river on March 23 with a force numbering nearly a hundred thousand men, supported by tremendous air and artillery bombardments plus the use of two paratroop divisions. Although Patton had not received permission for his attack, he was going

40

to employ his famous "rock soup" method to get his men across and engaged on the other bank.

Turning to the big map of the area, with its blue and red arrows indicating enemy and friendly troops, he stabbed a long thin forefinger at the village of Oppenheim, roughly midway between Mainz and Worms and commanded: "We'll cross here tomorrow night."

It was precisely 10:30 P.M. when the tiny assault boats of the 5th Infantry Division, commanded by Major General Stafford Irwin, pushed off into the darkness on the night of March 22. The night was perfectly still, save for the fire of the big guns far off. The operation was to be carried out without preliminary artillery or air bombardment to warn the unsuspecting Germans.

Meanwhile, farther north, two SS regiments waiting for the expected crossing of the Amis at Mainz were kept fooled as to the American intention by persistent artillery fire and a smoke screen laid across the Rhine. Thus while SS troopers stared, red-eyed and sleepless into the smoky gloom, the infantry doughs of the 5th crossed in their rubber boats and started to spread inland with only a handful of casualties.

By the time dawn broke and the surprised Germans began to react more vigorously, six battalions of infantry were across, plus several amphibious tanks. By noon the entire 5th Division was across and the construction of pontoon bridges was well under way. Patton greeted the news from Eddy like a mischievous child who now expected to be punished for having pulled such a trick— without orders and in advance of the official Montgomery crossing.

Bradley was just finishing his second cup of breakfast coffee when Patton called. "Brad," he said, with subdued yet barely concealed glee in his voice, "don't tell anyone, but I'm across."

Bradley nearly choked on his coffee. "Well, I'll be damned," he spluttered. "You mean across the Rhine?"

"Sure am. I sneaked a division over last night. But there are so few Krauts around there they don't know it yet. So don't make any announcement. We'll keep it a secret until we see how it goes."

A couple of hours later, during the daily morning briefing, Lieutenant Colonel Richard Stillman, Third Army liaison officer at Bradley's HQ, spelled out the details of the new Patton coup. With a smile he alluded to Montgomery's enormous preparations for the Rhine crossing and said: "Without benefit of aerial bombardment, ground smoke, artillery preparation and airborne assistance, the Third Army at 2200 hours, Thursday evening, March 22, crossed the Rhine River."

But while he was saying those very words, the Germans started to react. Angered at the way that Patton had tricked them, they threw in some of their last planes—the feared jet fighter-bombers, which had started to appear over the sky in West Germany and against which the fastest Allied fighter was lamentably slow. One hundred and fifty planes flew bombing or strafing runs against the advancing Americans and their bridgehead. The news brought Patton to the telephone once again.

Just after dark he called Bradley at the latter's HQ. Now he was no longer shy and hesitant. Now he was shouting the news over the telephone. "Brad, for God's sake," he screamed in that oddly high-pitched voice of his, "tell the world we're across! We knocked down 33 Krauts today when they came after our pontoon bridges. I want the world to know Third Army made it before Montgomery starts across."[1]

Patton, accompanied by General Eddy, his tall, handsome aide Colonel Codman and hard-faced, tough-looking Major Stiller, of whom we shall soon hear much more, had

---

[1] In connection with this crossing, Patton wrote in his memoirs: "A somewhat amusing incident is alleged to have happened. The 21st Army Group was supposed to cross the Rhine on March 24 and in order to be ready for this earthshaking event, Mr. Churchill wrote a speech congratulating Field Marshal Montgomery on the *first* assault crossing over the Rhine in modern history. This speech was recorded and through some error on the part of the British Broadcasting Corporation was broadcast, in spite of the fact that the Third Army had been across for some 36 hours."

staged his own crossing of the Rhine River on the very day that Montgomery, the hated rival, was about to put his grandiose plan into operation.

Patton's manner was casual as he led the little procession across the low-lying pontoon bridge, but those who knew him could tell from the look on his face that he was up to something. Suddenly he stopped. "Time out for a short halt," he commanded. Obediently the procession halted. While the others watched him a little bewildered, General Patton sauntered in his gleaming riding boots to the bridge's edge and peered over at the slow-moving current of Europe's greatest river.

Then to the tune of the artillery barrage somewhere up ahead, and to the amazement of the others, he slowly undid his fly and thereupon urinated into the Rhine. His nephew Fred Ayer put it nicely: "This was the time that George Patton did piss in the Rhine and have his photo taken to prove it."[2]

Turning with a malicious grin on his features, he did up his fly and said, "I have been looking forward to this for a long time."

Then he walked to the other side of the bridge where it met the grassy river bank which the tanks had churned up into a mess of mud and sand. As he stepped off the last pontoon he appeared to stumble, sinking to one knee before finally steadying himself against the bank with both hands. When he rose, he extended his fingers, allowing two handfuls of muddy earth to drop to the ground. "Thus William the Conqueror,"[3] he said solemnly, a ham actor to the end.

George Patton was across the Rhine. Hammelburg lay ninety miles away.

---

[2] Just prior to this incident Patton had been ordered by Washington to make his reports less informal and slangy. That day he sent in a report which was the epitome of military writing. But it contained a PS. "This day I pissed in the Rhine."

[3] According to the legend, when William the Conqueror was landing at Hastings, England in 1066, he stumbled and fell. Realizing that his men would regard the fall as a bad omen, he quickly seized two handfuls of earth and said: "See, I have taken England with both hands."

Patton's victorious Third Army raced across central Germany at a giddy rollicking pace—sometimes as much as thirty miles a day. It was like a great race. The speed was contagious, heady with the feeling that nothing could now stop the triumphant, sunburned laughing young men, as they stood in the turrets of their Shermans or clung to the shaking sides of their half-tracks. *Nothing could stop them now!*

Facing them and the other Allied armies that March were more than sixty German divisions, but many of their formations were divisions in name only with fewer than 5,000 men apiece instead of the customary 12,000. In fact, Allied intelligence believed that there were barely 20 completely manned and equipped divisions left in the West, and even those lacked mobility because they did not have sufficient transport. In addition, there were splintered SS groups, "burned out" divisions (as the enemy called the survivors of a badly hit division), the Volksturm,[4] and thousands of able-bodied but poorly trained Luftwaffe men who were now conscripted to fight as infantry. As Cornelius Ryan has put it: "Disorganized, lacking communication and often competent leaders, the German Army was unable to stop or even slow up the systematic onslaught of Eisenhower's armies."[5]

The German field commander Blumentritt wrote after the war:

> The battles now beginning east of the Rhine were often obscure to us. Without an air force and with only a few tanks, without supplies we could no longer fight as ably as formerly. The means of communications failed, there was often no communication with the corps and divisions of the Army and many units had to act independently. Also communication with the higher echelons of command grew worse and worse. For days no orders came, often the sectors of the Army were suddenly altered, divisions were taken away, new units brought up. Firm tactical leadership was no longer possible, reconnaissance failed to an increas-

---

[4] A force mobilized from old men and youths on the civilian front, given a few hours training and then sent to the front to back up the regular troops.
[5] *The Battle for Berlin.*

ing extent and *we frequently did not know where the enemy was* [author's italics].

Blumentritt's boss, Field Marshal Kesselring, who had taken over as Commander in Chief in the West on March 1 and who had announced cynically to his new staff on that day, "Well, gentlemen, here I am, the new V-3,"[6] was even more explicit. He wrote:

The enormously costly battles of the last half year and the constant retreat and defeat had reduced officer and men to a dangerous state of exhaustion. Many officers were nervous wrecks, others affected in health, others simply incompetent, while there was a dangerous shortage of junior officers. Furthermore symptoms of disintegration were perceptible behind the front which gave cause for uneasiness. The number of "missing" was a disquieting indication that a rot was setting in. The attitude of the civilian population in several districts . . . confirmed the tendency. Even among military staffs political talk could be heard which undermined the solidarity of resistance and nourished defeatism at the lower levels.

Thus into the wake of wildly retreating Germans came the victorious Americans, at their fore, Patton's Third Army. Pushing on at a tremendous, exhausting pace, they penetrated the extremely hilly and wooded countryside on the other side of the Rhine. Here each hollow seemed to contain a small ancient village of decrepit half-timbered houses, sleeping dustily in the hot spring sun; the only sign of life the white bed sheets, towels, nightshirts flapping lazily in the soft breeze and indicating that yet another place was prepared to surrender.

When the troops reached the German Autobahns, the best roads in Europe, the speed increased even more and on one glorious spring day the infantry were treated to the sight of Patton's two crack armored divisions, the 6th and the 4th, racing down both sides of the great German road neck and neck!

The war seemed about over. Now the GI's were in-

6 V-1 and V-2 were the German missiles, first used against London in 1944-45. The V-3 was reputedly another terrible secret weapon that Hitler was keeping up his sleeve and with which he would win the final victory.

terested in three things only: women, booze and loot! Risking the sixty-five-dollar fine that Eisenhower had ordered clapped on anyone who even *spoke* to a German, they stood in the sunny, dusty, ancient cobbled street of the picture-book Hessian and Franconian villages, from which many of their anecstors had come long ago, waving their chocolate bars and packs of Lucky Strike, trying to entice the women to go into the backs of the trucks with them: *"You, chocolate—me schlafen."*

Colonel Codman, General Patton's aide, records how one day they were barreling along a road in a jeep when they came across an idyllic scene: two GI's breathing "down the neck of two not undecorative young ladies."

" 'Stop,' the General roared.

"Screeching of hot rubber as we slewed to the grassy side of the *Autobahn*.

" 'What the so-and-so do you mean by fraternizing with those so-and-so German so-and-so's?'

"The more self-possessed of the GI's unwound himself from his partner. 'Sir,' he said, 'these are two Russian ladies who have lost their way. We are trying to learn their language so as to direct them properly.'

"For a moment the General glared in silence.

" 'O.K.' he said, turning away, 'you win.'

"Then to Mins (his driver), 'Go ahead.'

"Out of earshot he relaxed.

" 'That,' he murmured, and there was admiration in his tone, 'is really a new one.' "[7]

When the speeding convoys halted for a brief stop at one of the higgedly-piggedly fairy tale villages with the low cottages and few turreted villas that looked as if they had no windows, the laughing, jostling infantry dropped into the dusty road and soon were swarming everywhere in the narrow, crooked, sun-drenched streets. Opening gates, venturing into back yards for chickens and eggs, smashing down the doors of locked houses with their rifle butts in

---

[7] Patton did not believe in the anti-fraternization laws. As he once said: "Anything my men have fought to capture, they are, by God, entitled to." This plus condoms and penicillin kept the Army's morale high and their V.D. rate low.

search of liquor and loot, they were like school kids gone wild. When they met others from their own company, they would yell, "This place bin looted yet?" And if the answer was in the negative, they would troop into the house with a whoop, pushing aside the frightened, black-clad old women and cussing them out with a mild, laughing, "What ya bitchin' about? Go on, ya old bastard—git! *Raus, raus!*"

Then the whistles would sound. The red-faced, angry, senior noncoms would bellow their orders. And out they would come. Flushed with drink and excitement, clutching their bottles of looted wine, captured German policemen's helmets, boxes of cigars, they would crowd into the waiting trucks and half-tracks ready to take them on for their next date with destiny on that mad, hectic rush into the heart of a dying country.

But the advance was not all beer and skittles. Here and there were still the fanatics—the little group of SS men, beardless Hitler youths and hard-faced experienced officer groups who had fought from Sedan to Stalingrad and back and who would never surrender, but would fight to the end. The war was their life, part and parcel of their existence; they had grown up against its violent, bloody background—they did not want to survive it. They fought a bitter, cunning, treacherous little war of their own: the ambush of a supply column on the secondary road leaving the drivers dead over their wheels; the Sherman surprised by the Panzerfaust[8] crew as it tried to grind its way out of the bog; the tented hospital suddenly taken in the middle of night a score of miles behind the front.

Leslie Atwell records such an incident, completely useless in itself, but one which as he puts it, "stands out as one of the more ghastly episodes of the war."

We were advancing down a road in convoy when a German tank drove out of a group of trees, fired point-blank, killed two of our men and then retreated from sight again. The convoy halted and two of our rifle companies went forward and surrounded the little grove that contained, they discovered, a platoon of German soldiers in deep foxholes. The German tank kept swivelling and firing, and after a

---

[8]The German equivalent of the bazooka.

while four of our own tanks came up. Each from a different direction sprayed the tiny stretch of woods with long
streams of flaming gasoline. Within a few seconds the
place became in inferno, and the shrieks and screams of
the Germans could be heard through the high curtains of
fire. A few, in flames, tried to crawl through, but they were
mowed down by our machine guns. Within a half hour we
went and on what was left of the little wood was a deep
bed of glowing golden coals, hideous to see and think about
in the spring sunlight . . .

It was against this background, then—this mixture of
triumph and tragedy—that General George Patton made
his fatal decision.[9]

A few days before—after the 3rd had stormed the
Mainz-Frankfurt-Darmstadt triangle—the Supreme Commander himself, General Eisenhower, had made a surprise
appearance at Patton's HQ. He had asked to be taken
into the morning briefing session and, when it was over,
had risen to make an impromptu speech to a startled group
of staff officers.

He pulled out all the stops. Beginning by saying that the
3rd Army was composed of seasoned veterans, he said
they had become blunted by their own greatness. He urged
officers and NCO's alike to be "more cocky and boastful"
because otherwise, he said, "people wouldn't realize just
how good the American soldier is." He mentioned spe-
cifically General Hugh Gaffey's 4th Armored Division
which had been stalled at the Nahe River near Bad Kreuznach before it had secured a crossing and which had been
criticized by the press because of the delay. With heat in

---

[9]At this time, Patton himself knew that although the back of the
German resistance was broken, there were still plenty of fanatics
ready to fight to the death. Up in the Ruhr, his old friend General
Rose had been ambushed and when he had offered to surrender
had been shot dead by SS troops. Closer to him, Col. Hines, son
of his old friend General Hines, had been struck in the face by
a solid AP shell and had lost both eyes and much of his lower
face in the attack on Frankfurt airport. And even as late as the
last week of March, a 4th Armored Div. hospital had been re-
taken by a surprise attack carried out by SS troops and held
captive for 48 hours.

his voice, Ike said: "But Goddamnit, they didn't mention the fact that the 4th Armored had been held up on account of the unprecedented speed with which it had advanced!"

Then his anger vanished. Turning to Patton with that famous wide smile on his broad face, he said he was not only a great general and a good one, but also a "damned lucky stiff." It was an ideal combination, for "did not Napoleon say that he preferred luck to greatness?"

Patton was so astonished by the praise that he later recorded the event in his diary, concluding with the entry: "I told him that this was the first time he had ever complimented me in the two and half years we had served together."[10]

We have no record of Eisenhower's reply.

So here was Patton at the height of his power, with hundreds of thousands of tough, aggressive men and a mighty mechanical war machine at his disposal to do with almost what he liked, now that Eisenhower had given him such fulsome praise. It is not surprising that he lost his sense of reality long enough to make *the* decision. For many, a man such as Patton, the great commander, is an outsize romantic figure. As in days of old, he stands—figuratively speaking—on a height, dominating the destinies of the many lesser figures, the ants, down below. Above fear and never concerned with the outcome of his decisions which can send so many men to their deaths, Patton and many a general like him appears to be unique. *But he isn't!*

As a necessarily anonymous British staff officer once remarked cynically, "Even generals sometimes wet their knickers."

Patton was *not* unique. Neither was he omnipotent nor omniscient—whatever his later-day apologists may say to

---

[10] Afterward Patton said to Gay, his chief of staff: "I think Ike had a good day. They ought to let him out oftener." "What I can't get over," Gay replied, "was his statement to the effect that Third Army isn't cocky enough. How do you explain it?" Patton stirred his soup. "That's easy. Before long Ike will be running for President. Third Army represents a lot of votes." When the others smiled, Patton said sharply, "You thinking I'm joking. I'm not. Just wait and see."

the contrary. Patton had his weaknesses—as we have already seen—just as have other men.[11] He was brash, impetuous, unconcerned with the petty cares of lesser men, and determined to have his way whatever the cost.

As he once remarked himself to his nephew Fred Ayer: "You have to be single-minded, drive only for the one thing on which you have decided. Then you'll find that you'll make some people miserable . . . And if it looks as if you might be getting there, all kinds of people, including some you thought were your loyal friends, will suddenly show up doing their hypocritical Goddamnedst to trip you, blacken you, and break your spirit . . ."

In that last week of March, Patton, in his single-mindedness, was to decide on a venture that would be the first step on that steep road to his downfall and death six months later. It was a step that, as General Bradley, his boss, later put it: "Began as a wild goose chase and ended as a tragedy."

---

[11] A good example of Patton's pettiness was his standing feud with Sergeant Bill Mauldin, the cartoonist creator of the two scruffy soldiers Willy and Joe for the Army paper *Stars and Stripes*. Starting with the soldier-editor of the *Stars and Stripes* and working his way right up to Eisenhower himself, Patton urged that either Mauldin have his characters shaved or he be sent back to the line. (Mauldin had been wounded with the 45th Div. in Italy.) Eisenhower laughed in Patton's face.

Chapter 5

On the morning of March 24, 1945, General George Patton's most famous division—the elite 4th Armored—lay stretched out along the western bank of the swift-flowing River Main, covering an area of twenty miles from the town of Aschaffenburg in the south to Hanau in the north. Soon the division's Combat Command A was scheduled to cross the river at Hanau while Combat Command B, under the aggressive leadership of Colonel Abrams, which had just seized a railway bridge across the Main a couple of miles south of Aschaffenburg, was under orders to cross there.

But on that particular fine March morning, with the sun a full pale gold in the crisp spring sky, the 4th Armored Division was not feeling very aggressive. It had been on the move for days on end by now, covering sometimes a score or more miles a day, chasing the fleeing enemy as he pulled back from the Rhine to the next water barrier, the Main. Now the tankers and armored infantry were exhausted.

On that morning they took advantage of the brief respite from combat. Those who could got their heads down in their battered dust-covered tanks, trucks and half-tracks and slept. Others stripped in the fields that bordered the river and washed themselves as best they could using their helmets. Here and there an amateur barber tried his hand at trimming the hair of his comrades, who sat naked to the waist, reading copies of the *Stars and Stripes* of March 21 which had just caught up with them. The paper featured a mock interview with a group of GI's who were mad about mechanical drawings.

"Ah, come on fellas, let's hit that detail," pleaded the sergeant, without response. They just lay there and mooned.

"It's no use," the sarge confided, "they've been that way ever since last night at the movies they saw a training film, 'Workings of the Super-Clutchable High Tension Generator with Engageable Gears.' I tell you, the guys fell in love with that machine."

"Ummmmm," sighed a six-foot private deliriously, "when I think of those ravishing camshafts, it goes to my head."

But the mock interview only raised a few halfhearted laughs. The men of the 4th were too worn and weary for humor. All they wanted was sleep.

The 4th, the only division apart from the 101st Airborne to receive a Presidential citation during World War II, had had a tough campaign, which although it had won the 4th the greatest record of any U.S. armored formation, had also worn it out.

Formed in 1942 under the command of General Wood, a tough commander whose idea of fun was to strip to the waist and roll in the snow in midwinter, it had been alerted for overseas service in November 1943. Then Wood had told his men, "If an order is ever given to fall back, that order will not come from me," and that promise was faithfully stuck to from the day the division went into action till the day the war ended.

On D plus 36, the final day of July 1944, the 4th Armored Division snapped into action for the very first time. Tearing a hole in the defenses of the German Seventh Army facing it, the 4th barreled across the Brittany Peninsula with the rest of the Third Army following it. The German line broke. In seven days it dashed two hundred miles across France to the Atlantic Coast. It was a tremendous drive, but only an augur of what yet was to come.

Patton next ordered Wood to rush for the Siegfried Line in faraway Germany, reiterating as he had done so often before: "Just keep going and don't worry about your flanks."

Wood needed no urging.

He tore forward sixty miles east of Paris even before the first Allied troops got within shooting range of the capital's suburbs. His tankers shot into the French town of Lens, with the gunners firing to left and right as they clattered down the cobbled streets like bad men in an old Hollywood B-type movie.

On to Troyes with Wood urging his subordinate commanders to further deeds of wild daring. "Keep going, keep going," he repeated constantly. "Don't stop. The enemy rear is our back yard!" And his leaders—Abrams, Generals Bruce Clarke and Holmes Dager among them—did not need to be told twice. Clarke,[1] whose motto it was that "tanks are a weapon of terror . . . in fact, the safest place to be in this war is behind the enemy line," rushed on, followed by chubby cigar-chomping Abrams, who led his 37th Tank Battalion from the point tank. On and on and on . . .

Quickly the division developed a style of fighting and cocky attitude all its own. It was fast and furious and based on fast aggressive shooting. The division's front was limited to the width of the roads down which its Shermans rumbled. In front, the reconnaissance element kept going until the situation became too hot for it to handle alone. Then the armored infantry swung into action, pressing their attack recklessly under covering artillery fire and coming in from the flanks. They either broke the enemy or flowed round his positions from both sides. There they cut his lines of communications and split up his major units. It was a costly method of attack, but it paid dividends and that was all that mattered to Wood.

As for his own flanks, they were the least of the tough, barrel-chested general's worries. He simply ignored them. As Sergeant Klinga of the 8th Tank Battalion put it in mock dismay while his battalion was "resting" miles behind the German lines. "They've got us surrounded again, the poor bastards!"

Sergeant Klinga, the coiner of that immortal statement, did not survive the war. Nor did 10,000 other members

---

[1]Clarke, like Abrams, also became a four-star general and an army commander.

of the division. Tough General Wood himself lasted only 90 days before the strain became too much for him and he had to be relieved by General Gaffey, who was every bit as daring. But in spite of the high casualties it took— the highest of any armored outfit in the European Theater —the "Breakthrough Division" or the "Devil's Pitchfork" as it was called,[2] soon acquired a reputation for extreme daring (foolhardiness, some critics said) and bold, independent action far ahead of the main body of the Third Army.

In the third week of December 1944 the division's career reached its peak. That week the situation on the Allied front was very grim. The Germans had broken through in the Ardennes and neatly divided the American command in two. In the middle of their panzer drive to the River Meuse lay the Belgian town of Bastogne, a vital road and rail center, now surrounded by the Germans, who outnumbered the "battered bastards of Bastogne"—the 101st Airborne—three to one. Patton was called in to help.

Ordering the 4th into action, Patton directed it to travel 200 miles from its positions in the Saar over murderously icy roads until it reached a spot suitable for striking against Bastogne. A little over 24 hours later the divisional attack kicked off on the one narrow cobbled road which led to Bastogne. They took village after village in bloody little actions, their tanks sliding over the icy roads like uncontrolled sleds. The enemy fought back desperately. All Christmas Day was spent in action, the armored infantry dyeing the snow red with their blood, the tanks and halftracks blazing fiercely against a leaden winter sky. Hundreds died on both sides. The 4th battled on.

On December 26 CCR launched a desperate attack on the village of Assenois, one of the keys to Bastogne. It was defended by a fanatical SS unit, determined to fight to the end. Led by Abrams, in the point tank as usual, the Germans and the Americans locked in bloody, fierce combat all day long, swaying back and forth until when evening

---

[2] "Pitchfork" because of its two-pronged typical attack formation.

came the whole village was in flames and a 100 battered tanks and half-tracks lay smoldering in the fields all around Assenois. But by that time the 4th had broken through the German perimeter and was on the inner road to Bastogne.

In the point tank Lieutenant Charles Boggess gave his driver rigid orders to keep his foot down hard on the gas pedal and thus they clattered up the road, Corporal Dickerman, the gunner, firing the whole while. Then at 5:00 P.M. the young officer spotted a foxhole armed with a machine gun covering the road. He ordered his driver to stop and then yelled, "Okay, you guys, you can come out. The party is over. This is the 4th Armored!" The 4th had linked up with the 101st Airborne.

That grim December meeting had been the high watershed of the 4th Armored Division's combat career. It still possessed a fine reputation, but a lot of the old spirit was gone. There had been too many casualties, the winter had been too long and too costly, and the drive through the Palatinate and on over the Rhine too fast and exhausting. The old 4th had vanished in the December mud. In its place was a collection of replacements, culled from less aggressive arms of the service, many of whom had never even seen the inside of a tank before. The division began to slow up. It bogged down badly at Bad Kreuznach and Gaffey, a personal friend of Patton's had to go, to be replaced by an "outsider" from another army, General William Hoge; it was the third change of command in less than ten months.

Thus, on that pleasant spring morning in March, 1945, the 4th was certainly an outfit to be reckoned with. But it was no longer the 4th that had fought in Brittany or at Bastogne. *That* division had died a good while back. Yet on that same March morning, while the men of the 4th slept or lazed in the spring sunshine, orders were on their way to them in the person of General George S. Patton, the execution of which would demand from them the same

spirit and dash they had once shown so long ago in the
sunny fields of France.[3]

That morning General Eddy, the commander of XII Corps
to which the 4th belonged, pondered over a strange order
he had just received from George Patton, his boss. He
didn't understand it and he *certainly* did not like it. As he
mulled over the implications, he had one of those sudden,
nauseating feelings that were becoming increasingly frequent this spring.

Burly, bespectacled Manton Eddy had been a regimental
officer since 1916, when as a young shavetail machine-gun
commander he had been posted to France where he had
seen much combat and been wounded. After the war, he
had worked himself up the ladder of command until he
had been promoted commander of the 9th Infantry Division and had fought it successfully through the North
African and Sicilian campaigns. Later he had received the
D.S.C. for his brave and aggressive leadership of the division at Cherbourg and been promoted to corps commander. But by March, 1945, he was a dying man and he
knew it. He was suffering from such high blood pressure
that those doctors who were in the know said he wouldn't
live long if he didn't have an operation.[4] Eddy ignored
the doctors. He was determined to stay in combat as long
as possible.

But on mornings like this he dearly wished that he had
given in to the demands of his doctors. As he reached for
the telephone, he felt the usual nauseating sense of sick-
ness and nervous pressure which he always felt these days

---

[3]In some battalions there had been 100 per cent turnover in
officers; and in the armored infantry companies there had been a
high rate of casualties, especially among the riflemen. The tankers
weren't exempt from losses either. The 37th Tank Battalion, for
instance, accepted one batch of replacements in December, *of
whom only two had ever seen the inside of a tank*—one of these
as a result of having once been given a ride by a cousin in the
Armored Force.
[4]A month later he was relieved of his command, flown to the States
and operated on in the nick of time.

when he had to pass on an order like the one he had just received from Patton.

Reluctantly, he picked up the telephone and got General Hoge, the new commander of the 4th on the line.

After a few hesitant preliminaries, he got down to business. Hoge might as well know as soon as possible what George expected. "Bill," he said, "George wants a special expedition sent behind the lines to pick up nine hundred prisoners at Hammelburg."

Then he started to fill Hoge in on the details.

At the other end, the tall, hard-faced, tough commander of the 4th listened intently, his blue eyes characteristically half closed. He said little. But after Eddy had gotten off the line, he sat there alone in his command post, wondering what Patton really expected of him by giving him such a task. He was new to the Third Army, but he knew Patton. Was this something dreamed up by George to test him? After all, he had been in charge of Patton's favorite armored division for only a matter of days. Did Patton expect him to refuse or contest the order? After all, Patton knew from Hoge's service reports and the scuttlebutt passed back and forth among senior regular army officers about Hoge's reputation for plain speaking, even when it meant reducing his chances of promotion. As he sat there, pondering the order, he concluded it was a very strange business indeed.

William Hoge had never tried to be popular, either with his men, his superiors or with the press. But in spite of that, he was respected and sometimes even liked as a tough, hard-hitting general who pulled no punches either with the enemy or with his own men. A graduate of West Point—as were his brothers and his two sons—he had fought in World War I. Thereafter, his achievements had been outstanding. He had been in charge of the pioneer stage of the Alcan Highway, supervised the unloading of supplies at Omaha Beach, fought his raw, inexperienced combat command of the 9th Armored Division with distinction at St.-Vith during the initial stages of the Battle of the Bulge, and had commanded the 9th Division team which had captured the famed Remagen Bridge, the first bridge won across the Rhine—*and this against strict and explicit orders not to do so!*[5]

Yet there was something about this tall, stern man with the black hair and hard eyes that mitigated against him. He could not tolerate weakness or deceit and was outspoken when he encountered them. Perhaps he was too frank, too outspoken, but whatever the reason, men of far less ability and experience had long been promoted over his head. Now, a few days after he had at long, long last received his first divisional appointment, Patton had given him an impossible task like this. *What was he going to do?*

General Hoge did not have a long time to ponder what he was going to do. Only a matter of hours later Hoge was surprisedly informed by an aide that the Army commander himself wished to speak to him. Hurriedly he seized the phone and said "Hoge."

Patton's voice was pitched even higher than usual. In a flow of nervous, rapid sentences, he gave Hoge further details of how the Hammelburg raid should be executed. He ended on a triumphant note, eager as ever to do some other general in the eye, be he German or Allied. "This is going to make the MacArthur raid on Cabanuatun look like peanuts, Bill."[6]

Hoge did not argue with Patton. Patton wasn't the man to argue with lightly. Instead he called Eddy and gave him his feelings about the "raid," as Patton called it.

---

[5]Just before taking the bridge, Hoge had received a message from III Corps canceling the mission. Patton had broken through to the Rhine and Hoge was ordered to drive south at once and join up with him at Koblenz. It was a blow. Before Hoge lay the great opportunity of his war. He hesitated only momentarily. It was a hard choice for a soldier. If he succeeded, he would be a hero. If he failed, he could well lose his command and ruin his military career. He decided to take the bridge and to hell with the consequences.

[6]A month earlier in the Philippines, that other U.S. commander with an eye for publicity, Douglas MacArthur, had gained considerable attention in the press by taking the POW camps at Santo Tomas and Bilibid in Manila and liberating 5,000 prisoners.

Quickly and logically he explained his reasons for disliking the undertaking. A task force sent on such a raid—Patton was talking in terms of a combat command—would weaken his already overextended, exhausted division. According to the book, a divisional front facing an enemy such as the German should not extend more than six miles. *His was stretched over twenty!* Besides, most of his men were exhausted—as Eddy knew—after a thirty-six hour, nonstop race to the River Main. His temper getting the better of him, he asked, "What's so darned important about Hammelburg and a handful of prisoners of war?"

At the other end Eddy listened attentively to his subordinate, then he said soothingly, "All right, Bill, I'll take it up with George."

A day passed. Then on the afternoon of the next day, March 25, a short, red-haired major in his forties was ushered into Hoge's headquarters. He was Major Alexander Stiller, one of Patton's senior aides.

Stiller had been one of Patton's original tank sergeants in World War I. Just before Patton had set sail for North Africa in 1942 he had received an unexpected telegram from his old sergeant, asking to be taken along. Patton answered in the affirmative, and a few days later Stiller had turned up in his old World War I uniform, complete with leggings and flat pancake helmet. Hastily he was refitted and joined the force sailing for Africa. Thereafter, he and Colonel Codman were regarded as Patton's closest associates, two men who were devoted body and soul to "Old Blood and Guts."

Hoge looked with a certain suspicion at the wiry Arizona cowboy and former Texas Ranger, who bore several notches on the butt of his forty-five to signify the number of men he had killed. But he said nothing while Stiller saluted and introduced himself. Then he asked the major what he wanted.

Stiller replied that he was going to go along on the raid.

"But I thought the idea was shelved," Hoge said, rising to his feet and looking at the other man in surprise.

"No, sir," drawled the tough, undersized Arizonan with

the leathery killer's face which his boss Patton had always envied. "The General wants it to go on as planned."

Hoge waited until Stiller had gone, then with a worried look on his face, he telephoned his corps commander Manton Eddy and asked him just what was going on.

Again Eddy was soothing. "Don't worry," he placated the irate divisional commander, "I'll handle the matter personally."

And with that Hoge had to be satisfied. The "Hammelburg affair" was becoming more and more curious. That night over his evening drink in the mess, General Hoge asked himself repeatedly what the hell it was all about.

He was soon to find out.

One day later a bustling, smartly uniformed General Patton, accompanied by thin handsome Colonel Codman, a former World War I pilot and himself a former German prisoner of war, arrived unexpectedly at General Eddy's forward headquarters.

They were on the way to visit Colonel Hines, the son of Patton's friend General Hines, who had just been struck in the face and blinded by a solid armor-piercing shell during the attack on Frankfurt airport. They were met by General Ralph Canine, Eddy's chief of staff. He was flustered and a little embarrassed that his boss wasn't there to meet the Army commander.

"Where's Matty?" Patton asked unceremoniously, as if he were in a great hurry, though later—much later—Canine began to feel that Patton had for his own reasons deliberately picked this moment when Eddy was absent.

"He's not here, sir," Canine answered hurriedly. "He didn't expect . . ."

Patton cut him short. "Pick up the phone and get Bill Hoge," he snapped impatiently. "And tell him to cross the Main River and get over to Hammelburg."

Canine hestitated. He knew Patton and his explosive temper. Feeling himself going red in the face, he stared at the Army commander, all glittering brass and polished leather, as the latter looked at him impatiently.

At last Canine plucked up enough courage to tell Patton

what his boss had told him to say should Patton appear: "General, the last thing Matt told me before he left was that if you came by and told us to issue that order, I was to tell you I wasn't to do it."

Abruptly he stopped, swallowed his own breath and waited for the hail of angry cuss words to descend upon him for such insubordination.

But none came.

There was no anger in those squinting blue eyes which had been known to make strong men quail with one sharp look.

"Get Hoge on the phone," Patton said softly, giving no indication that he was angry at such rank insubordination, "and I'll tell him myself."

Canine, still reluctant, yet pleased that he had not been forced to betray his own boss, did as he was ordered and a few moments later Patton was talking directly with the commander of the 4th Armored Division. Quickly Patton got down to business and ordered Hoge to carry out the plan as ordered.

Angry at last at this harebrained scheme of the Army commander, Bill Hoge protested that he couldn't spare a single man or vehicle; his division was exhausted and over-extended as it was.

Still Patton didn't lose his temper, as he so easily did under normal circumstances. Instead his voice took on an almost wheedling tone which surprised—even shocked—Hoge. In fact, the divisional commander was distinctly embarrassed by Patton's tone.

"Bill," he wheedled, "I promise I'll replace every man and every vehicle you lose . . . *I promise!*"

When Hoge put the telephone down he was completely bewildered. Again he asked himself the question which had been troubling him off and on for the last two days: *What the hell was so important about the prisoner-of-war camp at Hammelburg?*

In his bewilderment, he looked across at leathery-faced Major Al Stiller who had been listening on the other line. The latter hesitated, then finally explained what it was about to a shocked Hoge.

The "Old Man" wanted Hammelburg liberated because his own son-in-law Colonel John Waters was a prisoner of war there. That was the purpose of the whole raid.

Nothing more, nothing less.

General William Hoge looked at the little major in blank, utter amazement while, outside, the background music to the war, the artillery barrage, rumbled on unnoticed. So *that* was the reason!

Chapter 6

There is a marvelous picture still extant of the two men to whom Hoge gave the task of preparing the raid that Patton had forced upon him. It shows Colonel Creighton Abrams and Lieutenant Colonel Harold Cohen posed in front of a tank of the former's 37th Tank Battalion. The two colonels are both laughing as they stand there bareheaded, their hands clasped around a bottle of wine. Abrams' face is broad, fleshy, almost chubby and boyish, while that of Cohen is narrow and long, the steel-rimmed GI eyeglasses he is wearing thickly caked with the dust of France. The two men had fought side by side many a time when Abrams' tanks had worked together with Cohen's 10th Armored Infantry Battalion, and many of the former's triumphs, which had gained him the reputation for being one of the most aggressive tank commanders in the Army, were due to the armored infantry men of the 10th.

Now, after Abrams had learned that his CCB had been given the task of taking Hammelburg and that Eddy refused to let him send the whole combat command,[1] he thought that if anyone could take Hammelburg, it would be Hal Cohen. He telephoned him immediately after being refused by Hoge and gave him the prickly, danger-fraught task.

Cohen, a tall slim man, who was at once both elegant and exceedingly tough, was a wartime soldier who had abandoned the textile mill he owned in South Carolina to join the infantry rather than the Quartermaster Corps,

---

[1] Abrams had telephoned Hoge and told him that if the job had to be done, the whole of the CCB should go; a reinforced company would be wiped out. Hoge turned down his suggestion; Eddy had refused to divert the 3,000-man-strong combat command for the task.

where he might easily have found a soft, comfortable job using his expertise to provide uniforms for the fighting men.

After attending the Officers Candidate School, he was promoted quickly until he finally took over command of the 10th. This rapid promotion was partly due to his aggressive, fighting leadership; but it was also due to his ability to look ahead and prepare in advance for any sudden contingencies which might arise on the battlefield. It was a valuable gift. As Martin Blumenson says of him in his article on the raid:

> For the Hammelburg mission, which would test the ingenuity of the commander, and which would require flexibility, instant reaction and immediate response to a variety of unexpected situations, no one was better qualified to lead than Harold Cohen.

Thus it was that on that warm spring day Colonel Cohen got down to planning the raid in his usual methodical manner, and if he wondered why the operation was to be carried out, he kept his doubts to himself. A good soldier, he told himself, should not question orders but carry them out. That was one thing he'd learned in the 10th, do first and ask later. Yet it did seem strange that Patton's aide Stiller was going on the raid. Why? What was his function? Stiller gave no other explanation than that he was going along for the fun. Cohen had looked at him quizzically over the top of his GI glasses, but had said nothing. For fun, he thought scornfully. What a nut! Then he got back to his planning.

As we shall see later, Patton would do his level best to prevent the details of the Hammelburg raid being spread outside the inner circle of the Third Army, and when he failed in this, he would deny to the press, the public and his superiors that he had ordered the raid to free his favorite son-in-law, husband of his beloved daughter "Little B." When called to account by his boss General Bradley, he assured the latter that "he did not learn of his son-in-law's incarceration until nine days after the raid." Colonel Codman, Patton's senior aide, also believed firmly that his chief was unaware of Colonel Waters' presence in the camp until much later. He wrote after the war:

> From General Patch,[2] General Patton learned that among the inmates of the camp was his own son-in-law.

Fred Ayers, Patton's nephew, who questioned his uncle on the subject at the time, wrote also:

> I do not know whether Uncle George had known beforehand that John Waters was in the P.O.W. camp at Hammelburg. I do know that he told General Bradley that he was not aware of Waters' presence *till nine days later* when Hammelburg was recaptured by our forces. From experience in intelligence work,[3] I think he should be believed . . . I cannot remember a single instance, during those days of movement and confusion, when a command was aware of the identity of individual prisoners in any individual P.O.W. stockade of whose existence they had just learned.

Asked for an opinion on the subject, General Sir Kenneth Strong, Eisenhower's shrewd, capable chief intelligence officer at that time, writes:

> If the transfer (of Waters from Poland) took place when the fighting was on then I do not think Intelligence would have been able or had the time to follow it.

Yet after all is said and done, it nonetheless *does* seem that Patton knew where his son-in-law was in the last week in March and knew the location of Colonel John Waters from the highest military source in Europe, *from the Supreme Commander, General Dwight D. Eisenhower himself!*

John Toland, author of the best-selling *The Last 100 Days*, was the first to reveal this information in the chapter of his book devoted to "Task Force Baum." After questioning most of the participants in the high-level planning for the raid—Hoge, Canine, Abrams—he learned that:

> One month before three U.S. officers who had escaped from Poland to Russia told major General John Deane, head of the U.S. Military Mission in Moscow that Waters and other Yanks marched west. Deane wired the information to Eisenhower, who passed it on to Patton.

---

[2] Commander of the U.S. Seventh Army, whose lines were reached by a few survivors of the raid on April 4.
[3] Ayers was an F.B.I. agent.

It is probable that the officer who told Deane of Waters'
whereabout was a young lieutenant, Craig Campbell, who
had been captured at the same time as Waters at Kasserine
and who had been in the same camp in Poland. In this
context, it is worthy of note that Captain Butcher, Eisenhower's aide, notes in his diary for March 12, 1945:

> General Deane, head of the American Military Mission
> to Moscow has radioed that among American prisoners
> of war released by the Russians in their great advance
> is our friend and my brother aide, Lieutenant Craig Camp-
> bell, who had been captured in Tunisia during the battle
> of the Kasserine.

The fact that a former member of his staff had been
released would surely have attracted attention among the
closely knit group of the Supreme Commander's intimate
associates. One thing must have followed another until the
staff was able to pass on the news to Eisenhower that
Campbell had revealed the presence of Waters in the Polish
camp and that he had been forced to commence the long
march westward by his German captors.

*But how would the Allied authorities in the west have
known where Waters was, once he had left Poland?*

To me there seem to be possibilities. It is now well
known that both sides during World War II allowed
specified, highly trained troops to be *deliberately* captured
during combat so that they could report certain features of
prison-camp life back to their superiors at home, either by
a prearranged code used in their Red Cross letters to their
families or by the cunningly devised radios which were
constructed in virtually every prison camp on both sides
of the line. In 1943, for instance, the Germans planted a
high-ranking Gestapo officer in the Russian POW camp
at Lunjovo from where, disguised as a *Wehrmacht* major,
he reported for a whole year on the activities of the turn-
coat German generals captured at Stalingrad who went
over to the Russians. Before he was unmasked and shot,
this German had virtually sabotaged the whole operation.
One year later the Germans had also planted several similar agents in British POW camps in the United Kingdom,
and used them to organize the abortive December 16, 1944

prisoner-of-war revolt, which was timed to coincide with the start of Hitler's "Last Gamble"—the sneak attack in the Ardennes. And in this same context there are three recorded instances of senior British NCO's deliberately allowing themselves to be captured in 1944 in order to keep in touch with HQ on prisoner-of-war camp conditions by secret radio.

Now, we do know that Colonel Goode, the camp's senior officer, carried the parts of a secret radio in the bag of his precious bagpipes, but whether all these parts belonged to a receiver or a transmitter is no longer known. Knowing something of the mood of the Hammelburg prisoners at that time, I do not think they would have had either the initiative or the courage to risk severe punishment—possibly even death—for the sake of keeping in touch with their own troops who were, after all, so far away.

It is more likely that Patton, once he knew that Waters was heading westward with the group evacuated from the Polish prisoner-of-war camp, could find out where his son-in-law was through official channels. For instance, most of the prisoners evacuated from Poland passed through or near the Saxon town of Dresden or that local area. Between January 15 and 22, the local represenative of the Swiss Legation, the Protecting Power,[4] reported to the British government that seven large U.S. groups from Poland were passing through the town. One month later, a further visit to the town by the Swiss after the terrible raid on Dresden, revealed that there were 26,620 prisoners of war in the town including 2,207 Americans, evacuated from Poland.

Once the U.S. kriegies had crossed over the Elbe at Dresden, they were distributed to *Oflags,* (prison camps for officers) in that part of Germany still left unoccupied by the victorious Allies. By the beginning of March 1945, the number of *Oflags* still left available to the Germans was limited and confined to three major areas: west of the River Elbe below Hamburg; the area around Munich and

---

[4]During World War II Switzerland, a neutral country, was the Anglo-American protecting power, primarily concerned with protecting the interests of Anglo-American POW's in German hands.

farther south into Austria; and the Franconian area which included Hammelburg. By the third week of March there-fore—Waters arrived on March 8—it is not *inconceivable* that the International Red Cross (which had to be in-formed of any change of a prisoner-of-war's location and in addition, as we have seen, had representatives in Germany keeping tabs on the prisoners) would have registered Waters' presence in one of the few remaining Oflags, at Hammelburg. This information would have then been filed at its main headquarters in Geneva. For a man like Patton, with important U.S. and international connections, it would not surely have been too difficult to obtain the information about the location of his son-in-law's camp.[5]

For his part, General von Goeckel, the last commandant of Hammelburg and a man who should know, maintains that he felt right from the start that *this* was the only con-ceivable reason there could be for the daring and unique raid launched on what was otherwise a very small and un-important military target.[6]

And anyone who took part as a combat soldier in the 1944-45 campaign in Europe knows full well that no special provisions were made for the freeing of Allied prisoners of war, even when, as in some cases, their lives were known to be in danger. For the fighting soldier, the prisoner of war was usually a burden who held up the advance.

In this context the general writes:

---

[5] The man most likely to have helped Patton here was rotund George Allen, former Commissioner of the District of Columbia by appointment of President Roosevelt, and from 1942 Chairman of the Prisoner-of-War Committee of the U.S. Red Cross. "In this role [as Eisenhower writes of him, the two men became firm friends when Allen came to Europe in 1942], "he had the chief responsibility, working through the International Red Cross and the Swiss, of establishing lines of access and communication . . . to our men taken prisoner by the Nazis." Through Allen, Patton could have found out what he needed to know.
[6] A week later, for instance, when Patton was within striking distance of Moosberg POW Camp, containing 30,000 Allied POW's, he made no special attempt to break through to it, although it held his old friend and aide Major Al Stiller!

I visited several of my new prisoners [the survivors of the raid]. Among them was a major—in civilian life a farmer in Texas—who told me he wasn't the leader of the operation but the liaison officer with the American Third Army.[7] Whether the name Patton was mentioned or not, I can't remember, *but we were all convinced at that time that the operation had been conducted solely on Waters' behalf* [author's italics].

General von Goeckel's belief was strengthened by the fact that some years after the war he was visited by a former major on Patton's staff who told him that the American Army commander had known that his son-in-law was a Hammelburg POW when he ordered the raid. This belief was also held by several of the senior officers who were Waters' fellow prisoners at that time.

How otherwise could one explain Stiller's presence on the raid? Of the men in Baum's force he was the only one who would know Waters personally, and it would be his job to single out the man who meant so much to Patton's beloved daughter.[8] What else would his function be in an operation commanded by a much younger and junior officer? Why else risk the life of a middle-aged officer who had served Patton loyally in two wars and of whom Patton could say later when he was criticized for ordering the raid: "No one who knows me would believe that I'd sacrifice Stiller to save my own brother"?

But the most convincing evidence comes from Captain Abe Baum himself. In an interview given to Mr. Theodore Irwin of the 4th Armored Division in 1959 Baum states: *"Not till hours later* [after the raid had started] *did I learn that Patton's son-in-law, captured in Tunisia in 1943, was reported to be a prisoner at Hammelburg"* [author's italics].

In short, it appears today—twenty-five years after the event—that General George S. Patton Jr. ordered Hoge to raid Hammelburg, *not* for a valid military reason, but for

---

[7] Although the general got the American's profession confused, this was obviously Stiller.

[8] Patton was passionately concerned for the welfare of his children. As Fred Ayers writes: "Uncle George was sometimes almost violent in the defense of his children, especially his daughters whom he jealously protected against dangers real and imaginary."

a personal one. If that raid had been successful, the fact that Lieutenant Colonel Waters was one of the liberated prisoners would be ascribed to sheer chance and good luck. When the raid failed, however, Patton was constrained to hide the real reason for ordering it. Fortunately, the Supreme Commander was aware to some extent of the plan and would keep out of the affair till he no longer could keep out of it, leaving the job of punishing Patton to Bradley, who was later to tell Fred Ayers:

> Your uncle was very upset. I felt that he had made a mistake, but didn't criticize or reprimand him. Failure itself was more than enough punishment for George.

But in the first flush of his overconfident decision to take Hammelburg, Patton was prepared initially—till Eddy refused—to sanction risking the lives of 3,000 American soldiers to achieve his aim. Later, when Eddy had talked him into reducing that number to 300, without a single doubt or any feeling of hesitation about the correctness of his conduct, Old Blood and Guts was still prepared to send 300 men who had wives, sweethearts and mothers back in the States to almost certain death for the satisfaction of a highly personal whim—the rescue of his favorite son-in-law.

The history of World War II is full of instances of generals indulging themselves in luxuries far removed from the more humble things available to the rank and file. There are also other instances thankfully fewer—of generals ordering their men into action and possibly to their death for the sake of achieving personal prestige and honor. As anyone who has ever served in an army knows—"Rank hath its privileges."

Yet Patton's decision to attack Hammelburg to rescue Colonel Waters must be without parallel as the most selfish action of a commanding general in the entire course of World War II. And when it was all over and done with and he realized the full extent of his decision—its cost in human life and misery—not one word of regret ever crossed his lips for the men who had died to achieve his purpose. The only regret that was every wrung out of the hard old warrior was this statement in his memoirs:

I can say this, that throughout the campaign in Europe I know of no error I made except that of failing to send a Combat Command to take Hammelburg. Otherwise, my operations were, to me, strictly satisfactory.

And on that strictly military note, devoid of any human feeling, the "widow-maker" (as he had been known to call himself) had said his last word on the whole unhappy business.

But back at Cohen's headquarters on the Main, there was no time to waste on the reason for the operation. If the general wanted a raid, he would get it. Working against the clock, Cohen put together the task force. It would consist of a group built around a tank company from the 37th and an infantry company from his own 10th. The armored infantrymen would ride on the decks of the ten Shermans and six light tanks which would make up the force's armored spearhead. Behind them would come 27 half-tracks to carry the prisoners—if and when they were rescued—which were now to be loaded with as much spare gas as they could conceivably carry. Three assault guns would give added punch to the force if they bumped into anything that the 75-mm gun of the Shermans could not handle, such as a *Tiger* tank armed with its fearsome 88. Thus most of the vehicles were armored, though there were six soft-skinned peeps and a cargo-carrying Weasel in the force which numbered 53 vehicles and was manned by just over 300 officers and men.

Yet as Cohen worked feverishly that long March day to get the force together, he felt less and less capable of leading it himself. Bad, bleeding hemorrhoids, caused by the hypertension of command over the last nine months of combat and aggravated by the long jeep rides over the pitted, cobbled roads of Western Europe, were becoming increasingly worse. All through the 25th Harold Cohen sweated with pain, feeling himself about to faint half a dozen times. On the following day, he was forced to report sick. The medics had bad news for him. They insisted that he be hospitalized at once. He wouldn't be leading the expedition to Hammelburg after all. But who should now take command?[9]

On the afternoon of March 26, Captain Abraham Baum, former pattern cutter in a Bronx ladies' blouse factory and now S-2 of the 10th Armored Infantry, was asleep on the hood of a half-track. Captain Baum had nine months of combat behind him and by now was fully imbued with the 4th's fighting spirit. The rangy six-footer with the crew cut and mustache was, at twenty-four, a cocksure, aggressive leader who, as Martin Blumenson has said, "looked like a policeman . . . and was anything but subtle."

But if Abe Baum lacked Cohen's finesse, he shared the latter's toughness and combat know-how. The husky New Yorker had already earned a batch of medals and purple hearts during five campaigns. He was a shrewd, efficient fighting soldier who enjoyed the respect and loyalty of every man under him. His nickname, "Able," summed up his unquestionable military ability. As Martin Blumenson said of him: "He knew what the war was about and he was going about winning it in the most direct way he knew. His instincts were right and his training had been thorough. Nine months of combat had hardened him . . . he gave way to no one in the matter of guts."

Now he slept the sleep of an exhausted man. The battalion had been on the move for days, and in the last four he had averaged only one night of rest. But he was not to sleep for long. At about two in the afternoon he felt someone shaking him awake. Bleary-eyed and utterly drained of energy, he stared up at the fresh-faced young lieutenant who had awakened him, and muttered through dry, cracked lips, "What the hell is it?"

"Able, you're wanted at headquarters. The Old Man wants to speak to you," came the reply.

---

[9]But Cohen did not escape altogether the hazards faced by the Hammelburg force. At about the time that group had completed its task, the hospital to which he was sent—the 16th Field Hospital at Altenstadt—was seized and held by the 6th SS Mountain Division. Later, upon release, Cohen confessed he was "not so much scared as downright embarrassed" at being taken prisoner 70 miles behind the front.

Captain Baum rubbed his sore, reddened eyes and cursed violently. Could a man never get any sleep? Then he slid heavily to the ground. Seizing his helmet, he hurried to the fiery combat command chief's C.P.

Colonel Creighton Abrams was waiting for him, surrounded by his staff officers, including Harold Cohen and an elderly major with a tough leathery face, who wore campaign decorations from the Great War and who was new to the young armored captain.

Quickly the burly colonel got down to business while Baum tried to stifle a yawn—unsuccessfully.

"We have a special mission for you," Abrams snapped. "Orders come directly from General Patton."

He paused and let the full import of his words sink in as his eyes searched Baum's.

"You know where Hammelburg is?"

"Yes, sir," Baum answered, feeling his heart beat more quickly. He knew about Hammelburg all right. Not only had the rumor of a top-secret "suicide mission" to Hammelburg been kicking around corps and then division for a couple of days now, but he had done the detailed planning for it with Cohen the day before. "It's about sixty miles due east of here."

Abrams nodded. "Yes, there's a prisoner-of-war camp at Hammelburg. We want you to take a task force and liberate as many Americans as you can. We think there are about three hundred officers at the *Oflag*." The colonel hesitated. "The division is not to follow you—you'll be on your own. We'll give you the best we have available. You're to get back to us whichever way you can. You understand?"

Baum didn't speak.

Abrams looked hard at him. *"If anyone can get there, Able, you will,"* he said softly.

Baum snapped completely awake. It looked as if the project had landed fair and square in his own lap. Now that the ailing Cohen couldn't go himself, he had presumably passed the job over to him as the man next best suited for it. Yesterday he had thought the operation was on the risky side. The odds against it succeeding were too great. But he was flattered that Cohen had suggested him for the leadership and that Abrams had accepted the suggestion. Besides, he liked the direct action of command much better than sitting behind a desk at battalion headquarters shuffling papers, however important they might be.

Smiling, he turned round and cracked to his battalion commander, "This is no way to get rid of me. I'll be back."

Cohen and Abrams laughed and then started to give him detailed instructions. He was to take the most direct route to the camp, charging forward at top speed. If he met resistance, he was to bypass it if he could. Once he had liberated the camp, he was to load as many prisoners on his half-tracks as he could, and return. Other prisoners who were able to walk and willing to take the risk were to be given directions on how to get back to the U.S. lines and then be allowed to set out on foot as best they could.

Nodding every now and again and listening intently to Abrams' instructions, Baum found his eyes wandering over to the figure of the unfamiliar red-faced major. Who the heck was the guy?, he wondered curiously.

He was soon to find out. Finished with his briefing, Abrams turned to the new man and introduced him to Baum. "This is Major Stiller," he said. "He's from Third Army . . . he's going along with you."

Uneasily Baum waited until Stiller had moved away and then he asked Abrams directly, "What's the story?"

Hastily Abrams assured the young captain that Major Stiller would only be an observer from Third Army and that he would possess no command function, although he did outrank Baum. He went on to say that Patton was probably sending Stiller along in order to indoctrinate him into combat.[10]

Slightly mollified, Baum glanced over Abrams' shoulder at Stiller's tough sharp face with its thin, tight fighter's lips as the latter laughed with a group of other officers of the

---

[10]By this time Colonel Abrams knew Patton's secret. Although Stiller had told Cohen and other CCB officers that he was going along "for the laughs and the thrills," he had just admitted to Abrams in confidence: "I think Patton's son-in-law is in there."

Combat Command, and knew that Stiller was the last man in the world to need indoctrination into combat.

As Baum went out the door, an almost embarrassed silence fell on the little group of staff officers. Abrams looked hard at Stiller, who flushed a little. Angrily the colonel looked at the closed door and muttered, *"If this mission is accomplished, that guy deserves a Congressional Medal of Honor!"*

Then he bent over his maps again. Suddenly Stiller felt very much alone.

Once outside, Baum's confidence in his ability to lead the mission began to wane somewhat. Although he was very busy getting his men together and organizing the vehicles of his column, he still had mind enough to realize exactly what a tough nut he had taken on. Intelligence had predicted the raid would meet no opposition—at least at the start—but he knew too that Intelligence estimated that there were elements of two German divisions, one of them a Panzer division under the command of General Obstfelder on the other side of the River Main. Baum did not know what and where their strong points were. The terrain was pretty rugged too: steep wooded hills on one side of the main roads he would take and rivers on the other. He would have to cross at least two—perhaps even three—rivers. What if the Germans blew up the bridges in his face—or even worse—after him when he had gone over them? *Yes, what about the trip back?* With a bit of luck he might get through to Hammelburg without too much trouble because of the darkness and the fact that the German resistance might be paralyzed by the suddenness of his sneak attack, but wouldn't every damned German soldier and his brother in the area be alerted and waiting for the force to return?

His mood picked up a little when he briefed his officers on the job ahead. There were some pretty good men among them: Captain Lang, C.O. of "A" Company; First Lieutenant George Casteel, his executive officer; First Lieutenants Allan Moses and Elmer Sutton; Second Lieutenant

Norman Hoffner, in charge of the reconnaissance patrol. He didn't know the 37th's officers so well. But they looked pretty good to him. They were Second Lieutenant William Nutto, C.O. of the 37th's "C" Company; First Lieutenant Walter Wrolson, a maintenance officer; plus two patrol leaders, Second Lieutenants Raymond Keil and William Weaver. But the stalwart of the whole group was not an officer at all, but an enlisted man. He was Technical Sergeant Charles Graham, who had been with the 4th Armored right from the start when it was commissioned in Pine Camp. Graham was going to do tremendously fine work with his three assault guns before one by one they were put out of action in the last ditch fight which was soon to come. Baum was pleased to have him and his 105's along. Naturally he didn't know then that Graham was to be the only one of that little group who would escape back to his own lines under his own steam.

Thus the little force prepared for the tremendous adventure that lay ahead of them (though some of them still did not know where they were going, not even that they were going behind the enemy's line). More and more jerry cans of gas were stacked in the half-tracks. Metal cases of 75-mm and 105-mm ammunition were opened up and the gleaming yellow shells clipped in the racks of the Shermans and the assault guns. While the infantry cleaned and checked their Garands, the tankers tested the tension of their tank tracks and swung the turrets around to check whether the electrical turret system was functioning correctly.

Gradually their preparation for the hard battle ahead came to an end. Chow was served. Some ate ravenously as if to prepare themselves for the long night ahead; others hardly touched a bite. Here and there an old, combat-wise soldier stripped, washed and changed into clean GI underwear, knowing that if he were hit, he stood less chance of the dreaded gas gangrene infection if clean cloth was forced into the wound. The younger replacements, for their part, talked and joked a lot—perhaps far too much—a casual observer would have noticed that they went over to the edge of the road to urinate pretty frequently. Fear and nervousness were playing havoc with their bladders.

The hours passed by leadenly. Now it was dark. The talk and chatter had died away. The men, waiting in the dark column of vehicles, confined themselves to half-finished questions and grunted replies. Their cigarettes glowed in the spring darkness like a long line of fireflies. The only movement was that of the young replacements stepping over to the ditch to relieve themselves yet once again.

In the silent line of the 37th Tank Battalion vehicles, Tech 5 David Zeno of New York City glanced across at the stark outline of the railroad bridge silhouetted against the night sky and thought how strange that he of all people should be preparing to cross it by force of arms soon. *Why should it be happening to him?*

The thirty-year-old medic, isolated in his own particular mantle of darkness from his comrades, told himself it must be over fourteen years since he had last seen that bridge across the Main. He had been with "Poppa" on one of his periodic horse-trading trips. Soon afterward he had left Germany for good. He had been only sixteen but he had been old enough to know what the rising power of the Jew-baiting Nazi Party meant for a German-Jewish kid. He had fled to the States.

Once in the States he had survived the Depression working as a butcher in New York, had married and had just gotten on his feet when the war had come and with it "greetings" from his Uncle Sam. Soon afterward a some-what surprised Dave Zeno had found himself a cook in the U.S. Army. The soft job had lasted a year, cooking his favorite steak for the then Captain Abrams. But when the division had started taking heavy casualties in 1944, he had been remustered and had fought on that long bitter snowy road to Bastogne. A couple of months later his Weasel had been blown up at the Rhine and his body covered with shrapnel wounds.

After he had recovered he had been reassigned once **again**—this time as a darned medic. Now he and Andy

Demchak, his sidekick, were to be the sole two medics
with the column, responsible for the health and welfare of
the three hundred fighting men who were going along.

Just the two of them. No special supplies. No doc. What
if they took heavy casualties? Suddenly, as if in a vision,
Dave Zeno knew they would be hit—and hit bad. Ever
since he had been wounded on the Rhine, he could feel
that sort of thing, almost as if he had some kind of divining
device in his bones. He glanced again at the stark shape of
the iron railroad bridge and the dark waiting shore beyond
it and shuddered slightly.

Then he pulled himself together. So they were to take
Hammelburg. *Goddamit!* It was only a dozen miles away
from the village where he had been born. Hell, his Poppa
had taught German Army recruits marksmanship there in
the last year of the Great War. Four generations of Zenos
had been born and had died in the area, trading horses as
far east as Bulgaria and as far west as Holland. They had
felt themselves German, speaking the local dialect, drinking the good strong wines of the area, different only in that
they didn't worship in the same church as the others.

That was until Hitler appeared on the scene and the
Nazi Party started to grow in strength in Bavaria and
Franconia. When the brownshirts had started to spit on
Poppa in the open street of the cobbled main road of the
village in which he had been born, he knew it was time he
went. That had been 1930. Abruptly it struck Dave Zeno.
In a funny sort of a way he was going home. Surprised at
the strangeness of the thought, David Zeno laughed out
loud. All around him in the darkness his buddies looked at
him in bewilderment. *Going home . . .*

While the soldier Zeno ruminated about the past, Captain
Baum found himself looking at the luminous dial of his GI
watch with increasing frequency. Soon the whole weight of
the divisional artillery, hidden behind the hill, would open
up against the enemy-held village of Schweinheim—
"Swines home," one of the GI's had translated the German
for him—and then at 2100 hours precisely, the two "B"
companies of the 37th and the 10th would attack across the

bridge and into the village nestling in the two dark hill masses on the far side of the river. Then once the village had been taken a path freed for him, it would be his turn. *And then . . .*

He never had time to complete that thought. With a tremendous crash which made every man in the column jump nervously, the guns of the 22nd, 66th and 94th Armored Field Artillery Battalions opened and ripped the night sky apart with the horrifying noise of their shells. "Outgoing mail!" someone cried in the darkness, perhaps to reassure himself that it wasn't enemy firepower that had made the sudden startling and very frightening noise.

Captain Abe Baum did not hear the remark. He had just recalled what he had said to Cohen when he had been given the mission. Thinking of it now, he wondered if he had not spoken too soon: *This is no way to get rid of me. I'll be back.*

Part Two

The Forty-Eight Hours

☆☆☆☆☆☆☆☆☆☆☆☆☆☆☆☆☆☆☆☆☆☆☆☆☆☆☆☆

You frequently think everybody is against you, George, yet you have only one enemy in the whole world—*yourself!*I don't mean to sound like a Dutch uncle, but I told you innumerable times to count ten before you take any abrupt action. You persistently disregarded my advice, but it is not just advice any longer. Well, from now on, it's an order. Think before you leap, George, or you will have no one to blame but yourself for the consequences of your rashness.

GENERAL EISENHOWER TO GENERAL PATTON
(1944)

Chapter 7

2100 HRS
March 26 The attack started at precisely nine o'clock that night. At that moment the artillery barrage stopped and for one brief instant there was loud echoing silence. But only for one instant. On the hour the two "B" companies went into the attack, the armored infantrymen hugging the high ponderous rears of the Shermans as they rumbled cautiously forward in the darkness.

Intelligence had informed Abrams that his attack would meet with little or no resistance. Intelligence was wrong, as it so often was. Just as the lead tank had started to crawl hesitantly into the village of Schweinheim, the enemy reacted violently.

Suddenly the dark figure of a German bazookaman sprang up from the foxhole in which he had concealed himself, about one hundred yards in front of the first house on the cobbled village street. In one quick gesture the German had lifted up the Panzerfaust to his shoulder, aimed, fired and ducked into his foxhole again.

A thin angry stream of yellow and violet flame tore through the darkness, followed by a trail of red-hot sparks. There was the great hollow clang of metal on metal. The lead Sherman came to an abrupt halt, as if stopped by some gigantic invisible fist. For a moment nothing happened. Then there was the sudden sucking in of air, as if the stricken tank had lungs, and the Sherman went up in flames.

That first bazooka round was the signal for the rest of the hidden enemy to open up. Long low frightening bursts of Spandau fire hissed through the night air, their red and white tracer splattering the decks of the advancing tanks like a swarm of angry frustrated bees. The German tommy-gun—the Schmeisser—joined in with a mean hysterical screech. Everywhere the German bazookamen opened up with their one-shot suicide weapons.

Swiftly the Americans reacted. The infantry doubled forward at the crouch, keeping their heads well down to avoid the stream of bullets coming in their direction. Frantically the captain in charge of the tank company tried to get the first knocked-out Sherman on the radio. In vain. The lieutenant in command and his crew had bailed out. Giving vent to his rage in a long stream of curses, the C.O. called the next tank in the column and told the sergeant-commander to "get that f——g thing out of the way!"

The sergeant needed no urging. While he moved forward, firing his 76 and turret machine gun, swinging them from side to side and spraying the buildings on both sides, a man dropped from the hatch and started the knocked-out tank's engine. With a creak of protesting metal, the stricken Sherman limped to the side of the road. The way was free.

The infantry were in among the houses now. "Housecleaning" always meant sudden death and in the darkness it was doubly dangerous, but it had to be done if the Baum group was to get through. The foot soldiers ran to the first house. Swiftly the wooden door was kicked in. A grenade was lobbed. The inside of the kitchen exploded with a roar in a brilliant blinding flash of red and yellow. A sergeant shot forward, firing his grease gun from the hip. The kitchen was empty, save for a dead German lying in the debris of the floor. Raising his machine pistol, the sergeant fired a long rapid burst through the ceiling and then tackled the stairs. The first house was taken. But there were plenty more to come.

Meanwhile the tanks were advancing deeper and deeper into the village against increasing German infantry opposition. Corporal William Smith, who was there that night, describes what happened next:

> Our platoon moved in to clear the left side. The platoon leader's tank was hit and it blocked the street too. And the Krauts slipped in back of us and hit our rear tank with bazookas. We were trapped and I began to sweat.

But Smith had forgotten the armored infantry doughs of the 10th. Seeing that the tank boys were cut off and virtually defenseless against the attacks of the German bazookamen in the narrow street, "B" company rallied. With its captain at the head, the infantry battled their way forward, firing their Garands as they came. The Germans melted away.

Fighting desperately with the tank mechanism, the crew of the rear Sherman found they could still drive it. Frantically the driver flung the gear lever into reverse and with a deep throaty whine, it drove backward at top speed.

The fighting went on. Abrams had to fling in more men to clear the village for Baum. Midnight came and went. Still the road wasn't cleared. Back and forth the battle raged. By now several of the farm buildings were ablaze, bathing the scene of combat a bloody hellish red.

But let Corporal Smith take up the story again:

Nazis mounted the crippled tank ahead and began firing its 76 at us. The building beside us was hit and started to burn. Suddenly the company commander radioed we were to withdraw, because the task force had gone through. The burning building threw plenty of light so I put the tank in reverse and backed out the street. It was much safer now, but I was still sweating.

Now Baum's column of fifty-odd vehicles sped through the burning village. Vehicle after vehicle after vehicle rumbled safely over the one open cobbled street, the armored infantry ducking occasionally as an odd slug struck the side of their Sherman or another bazooka cracked and sent a violent red flame, two-foot-long, speeding through darkness. The sound of the fire-fight began to die away. The last half-track cleared the village. Up ahead the light reconnaissance tanks took over the point from the heavier Shermans. It was 2:30 in the morning. The night was dry and warm. There was a high overcast and no moon. Rapidly the column put on speed and started to drive due east. Behind them the battle died slowly away. The odd shell. The faint chatter of a Spandau. Then it stopped completely, save for the ever present rumble of the heavies far off in the distance. They were on their own now. No one behind them save the enemy. No one in front of them to whom they could turn for help. Ahead lay two divisions of enemy troops. Task Force Baum was on its way to one of the most desperate adventures of World War II.

Riding directly behind the light recon tanks and a little in front of Stiller in his car, Baum wondered what he was getting into. The silent, taciturn major had obviously not told him everything. There was something going on here about which he had his doubts. What it was, he couldn't figure out, but he *did* know that Abrams hadn't told him everything.

Riding in his command peep, preoccupied with the problem, young Able Baum suddenly felt—almost physically— that the German line had closed behind him. It was almost as if he knew it in his very bones: *the enemy had cut him off already . . .*

Able Baum had come from a good solid Jewish family, where one never cursed or indulged in vulgar behavior. When he had gone into the Army as an innocent, wide-eyed twenty-year-old, he had somehow expected that all Army officers would speak and behave like college professors (especially as he himself had never even completed high school). His first meeting with General George S. Patton in 1942 had soon disillusioned him about that.

Just prior to the general's departure for North Africa, he had addressed Baum's division at Fort Benning, beginning his speech with that immortal statement: "I want you men to remember that no bastard ever won a war by dying for his country. He won it by making the other poor dumb bastard die for his country." The profanity of the opening remark and what was to follow had so shocked Baum that he had groaned aloud to his neighbor, "My God, that's the man who is going to lead us in combat!"

Another shock came a little later when some stupid corporal looked at his papers and saw that in civilian life he had been a "pattern cutter." The NCO had not bothered to check what kind of pattern cutter he was and as a result the surprised Baum, who later admitted he couldn't even knock a nail in the wall, found himself transferred to the Corps of Engineers.

But Able Baum had survived the initial shocks of his Army career. He began to succeed. In spite of the fact that he hadn't even finished high school, he was sent to OCS and commissioned into the armored troops. In France in 1944, at 22-years of age, he had taken part in the 4th's tremendous dash across Brittany—two hundred miles in eight days. He had been hit by an enemy bazooka and blown up by a mine. In Belgium he had been one of the first men into Bastogne to be told by MacAuliffe that he and his men weren't needed. Returning to his starting off point after Bastogne was finally surrounded, he had been ordered to turn round and do the whole thing again—this time at the cost of many score casualties.

Now, in the spring of 1945, after nine long months of combat, he was no longer the naive Jewish boy of two years before. He was a tough, hard-bitten officer, who had gone through hell and survived. As a result he was a profane, somewhat cynical man, who had one loyalty and one mission in life: the loyalty to his division and its task of killing Germans. "It was really a very superior division," he could declare later. "The senior officers didn't care about the 'ring' [he meant the West Point class ring]. They were only concerned with fighting ability. And the men— they were tops, functioning best when they were surrounded."

But now young Able Baum was beginning to worry, for the first time since the campaign had started. Usually a man without imagination, Abrams' comment that the division was not going to follow him had made him realize that (as he said later) "the outfit had wiped me off straightaway." It had been planned that he should get through Schweinheim in thirty minutes; the battle for the German river village had taken five hours. Wouldn't that mean the Germans would be ready and waiting for him?

A suddenly worried Able Baum began to scan the dark woods anxiously.

But amazingly enough, Task Force Baum passed through the first five villages-Strass-Bessenbach, Keilburg, Frohenhofen, Laufach and Hain—with very little German opposition. The enemy was too surprised, it seemed, at the sudden appearance of the Yanks in their rear echelons. Occasionally a gush of flame, followed by a blinding shower of sparks showed where a German bazookaman had woken up to the danger a little too late, or a patter of machine-gun bullets like heavy summer rain on a tin out-house roof reminded the occupants of the vehicles which were struck that there was still an enemy out there in the darkness.

However, Baum wasn't taking any chances. He remembers that:

When we entered a town if we got any fire I gave the command to fire. I was right behind the lead tanks . . . All weapons were fired at suspicious places. No high explosive shells were fired from the tanks at night while passing through the towns because the column would have to stop.

All the same there were casualties, but Baum did not halt. He was under orders to keep going, come what may. He couldn't afford to halt, if he was going to get to Hammelburg—*and back*. If a man were badly shot up and was likely to die in one of the jolting, swaying White half-tracks, he was given first aid by the two medics with the group, Tech 5 David Zeno and Pfc. Andrew Demchak (both of whom were to win the Silver Star for their part in the raid) and placed gently on the roadside with a prayer that the Germans would find him when dawn came and give him medical care.

The column barreled on. Skirting strongly held Aschaffenburg, Task Force Baum turned east on the main road from that city to the small town of Lohr, set in the valley among high hills. Here the road entered a dense forest of tall, ancient oaks, intermingled with newer firs, planted in rigid, orderly lines with military precision. Typically Kraut, Baum thought, as they rumbled on, the sound of his tank treads resounding eerily among the trees.

By now his mood had brightened. After the success of

his drive through the last five villages at the cost of a handful of casualties, and supported by the knowledge that the speed of his movement had swept him past the occasional artillery piece covering the road before its crew could even man their weapon, he felt better. For the first time since he had learned of the Hammelburg operation on the 25th, he began to think that it might be almost practicable. For the first time he told himself he might really succeed in getting to far-off Hammelburg.

The first light of the false dawn flooded the sky a dirty white as the column entered the white-painted, red-roofed Hansel and Gretel town of Lohr, with the light tanks in the lead. Suddenly the first tank jammed on the brakes. A hastily erected barricade had been flung across the steep incline which led down into the town. Baum reacted swiftly. Calling up the Shermans which rumbled on immediately to the rear of his command peep, he ordered one of them to break down the hindrance.

Hastily Bill Nutto, in charge of the heavy tanks, sent up his lead tank while the long column ground to a halt and moved to the side of the road. The dust-covered Sherman, with its too high silhouette—a common and persistent cause of complaint among American tankers[1]—sped forward. But not for long.

There was a sudden flash of flame and the Sherman ground to a halt, a shining, smoking new metallic hole gouged in its side. It had been hit. *"Nazi Panzerfaust!"* someone yelled. Baum cursed. His first tank was knocked out already and he wasn't halfway to Hammelburg yet. But there was nothing he could do about it. Hurriedly the crew of the Sherman bailed out and transferred to a waiting half-track, while a second Sherman took over the task and swept away the barricade with a contemptuous blow from its high glacis plate, scattering the few defenders with a

---

[1]Despite official U.S. protests to the contrary, German tanks were consistently superior to the U.S. models throughout the war. In the main, this superiority was based on the quality of the German armor, the German gun caliber and the fact that every American tank model had far too high a silhouette.

single burst of its 50-mm machine gun. The column pressed on.

They were now rumbling down the main street of the little place. There was no time for reconnaissance. They would have to take their chance on getting through without opposition. Suddenly the commander of the lead tank's heart almost stopped beating. Crawling up the incline to meet him was a lumbering convoy of twelve camouflaged German Army vehicles!

The American reacted first. Before the unsuspecting Germans could awaken to the fact that the tank was enemy, the tank commander opened up with his 37–mm. cannon and single machine gun. Behind him the other light tanks followed suit, pouring a stream of vicious fire into the enemy "soft" vehicles which were completely unprotected. One after one the German trucks ground to a halt, slithering off the road at crazy angles, screams coming from inside as smoke began to pour from punctured engines. Without even stopping, the tanks plunged on, past the smoking twelve enemy vehicles which they had knocked out in so many minutes. As the half-tracks followed, a young officer staring with horrified fascination at the scene of death and destruction, noted that one truck contained a cargo of dying and dead women soldiers, their long blond and black hair flung free from beneath their gray peaked caps as they lay there in the smoldering wreckage. He gasped once. Then couldn't help himself. He vomited over the swaying steel side of the half-track.

The column roared on.

The force hit the River Main again. It was the eastern bank of the river, where it plunges in a broad S between Aschaffenburg and Wurzburg. Anxiously Baum regarded the new terrain. To his left lay high wooded hills; to his right was the river and, between it and the road, the railroad line which ran to the first big town he would hit—Gemünden. Before him lay a deep and dangerous-looking valley. He didn't like the setup one bit. Surely the Germans would be warned by this time? Soon it really would be dawn and the enemy would be able to see the real strength of his force. The road between him and Gemünden looked like the perfect place for a trap. He gave out the order that there was to be no talk and no use of the force's radio, but hardly had he given it when there came an excited burst of noise from the tanks in front of him.

An unsuspecting locomotive, dragging what looked like a collection of flat cars, was puffing down the line to meet him. It was too good a target to be missed. Baum grinned in spite of his mood. As he opened his mouth to yell an order to fire, the lead tanks opened up of their own accord.

The first round hit the locomotive fair and square in the side. It came to a shuddering halt. Smoke began to pour from its interior. A couple of scared engineers jumped from the cab and fled into the darkness. The tankers had scored their first victory against a train. But more were to come. A seemingly never-ending stream of trains was leaving Gemünden that morning.[2]

"All along the railway from the Lohr to Neuendorf, Langenprozelten and Gemünden were trains," Captain Baum recalled later. "I estimate there must have been about 12 trains, each consisting of 20 cars. It was just getting light and it was there that I realized I had run into something."

One after another the gleeful tankers in the lead shot up the unsuspecting German trains, laughing and chuckling among themselves—even after the exertions of the night—like a bunch of silly school kids. A flak train hove into view. The light tanks took after it like hawks after a hen. They roared up to the locomotive, punctured its metal sides with several rounds of 37-mm fire and left it spouting steam from several gleaming holes it didn't have five minutes before. The giggling infantry, getting into the spirit of the thing, joined in the fun by tossing thermite grenades at the stranded train as they themselves rolled by. The morning of March 27, 1945 was turning out to be a pretty bad one

---

[2] It is known now that the Gemünden yards were being used to unload troops for the Third Army front and that there were so many trains around just before dawn because an infantry division was unloading under cover of darkness; the only way they could avoid an allied air attack.

for the men of the *Deutsche Reichsbahn*. Within the space of an hour, the Baum force had disabled about half a dozen of the precious few locomotives still available to the hard-pressed German State Railway Service.

In return, as Baum remembers, "We got some 20-mm fire from Gemünden and from the other side of the train (in this case a big 30-car ack-ack train loaded with anti-aircraft weapons and concrete pillboxes), but they stopped firing as soon as the column really started rolling."

Now the long line of American vehicles began to approach the outskirts of the ancient town of Gemünden, which took its name from the fact that three rivers—the Main, the Sinn and the Saale—converged there.[3] Their approach was suddenly cautious. Baum once again gave the order for strict radio silence and as little talk as possible. The presence of so many trains gave him a clue to the size and importance of the place. If he could, he would have avoided the town, but he knew from his maps that it was on the most direct route to Hammelburg and he needed the small ancient bridge that crossed the River Saale before he could advance any further. Stopping the column in a bend in the road some five hundred yards from the bridge, he ordered Lieutenant Nutto to push his tanks forward into the town and take the bridge. With him was to go Lieutenant Sutton of the armored infantry. It was Sutton's task to take the houses on both sides of the road once Sutton had opened it up, and protect the road for the rest of the column to pass through.

As the two officers hurried away to get on with the job, Baum waited at the side of his peep with a grim-faced Major Stiller, saying nothing, but sensing a growing feeling of apprehension mount within him. The attack on Gemünden *could* mean the end of his Force even before it had really got started!

---

[3] *Gemünden* means "the mouthing," i.e., the meeting of rivers.

Chapter 8

0600 HRS March 27 As the combined infantry-tank attack started to move in on the three-river town of Gemünden just after dawn, luck was still on the side of the bold little American task force. Unknown to Baum, his rapid drive through Lohr had nearly overrun the command post of General von Obstfelder, the officer in charge of all troops in that area; although Obstfelder had escaped being killed or captured, his communications system with his subordinate units had been seriously disrupted.

So had those between Gemünden and the local corps command in the spiritual home of Nazism at Nuremberg. For the last few days low-level Allied fighter-bombers had tried to knock out the Gemünden marshaling yards. In vain. That morning the yards were still functioning. But if the bombers had failed to hit the railroad, they had put the local post office, with its military telephone installation, out of action—*exactly one day before the American task force arrived on the scene!*

It was a tremendous stroke of luck which Baum could not appreciate on that gloomy March morning as he stood on the narrow road outside Gemünden, searching the ancient church tower and ruined castle on the large hill in the center of the town for any sign of enemy activity while he waited for the first reports of the battle—which he knew must come—to start coming in.

He did not have to wait long!

The first reports began to flood in and they were all encouraging. The bridge across the River Saale was intact —and it didn't seem to be defended as far as the first recon patrol could make out. Baum rubbed the scruff of beard that had covered his face during the night, and

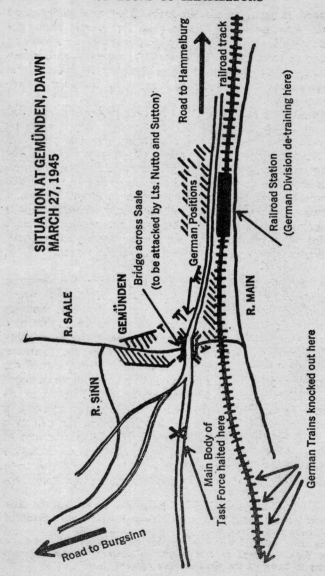

SITUATION AT GEMÜNDEN, DAWN
MARCH 27, 1945

R. SAALE

GEMÜNDEN

Bridge across Saale
(to be attacked by Lts. Nutto and Sutton)

German Positions

R. SINN

R. MAIN

Road to Hammelburg

railroad track

Railroad Station
(German Division de-training here)

Main Body of
Task Force halted here

German Trains knocked out here

Road to Burgsinn

grinned in spite of his tiredness. That was really good news! Another report. There were few people about yet and they all seemed absolutely bewildered to see American troops in their midst. Then another. There were German troops at the other side of the bridge after all. Baum could already hear the first single shots that heralded a fire-fight.

Quickly he poked his head into his command peep and got on to 4th Division's HQ. In a rapid, excited voice he reported that the bridge was standing, but defended, and he needed air support *urgently*. The faint voice at the other end said he would get it.[1] Baum felt a little less anxious now, but he would not have felt so relieved if he had known that the air support was never to arrive. In fact, it remains one of the mysteries of the whole expedition that it never really received any substantial air support, although Third Army invariably got air support readily and without difficulty from its attached Tactical Air Command.[2]

Up front, Sergeant Donald Yoerck, driving his Sherman cautiously into the Frankfurter Strasse, which led toward the bridge, was amazed to see a few early risers walking to work, briefcases in hand, completely unaware that in a few seconds they were going to be involved in a bitter little battle. In the tank in front of Yoerck's, Corporal Frank Malinski spotted a train steaming slowly out of the station toward his tank. Malinski did not hesitate one second. His 76 mm cracked into action! The Sherman shuddered. A hundred or so yards away the train came to a sudden grinding halt. Steam flooded out of the cab in a thick white cloud. Malinski pumped another round into it. And another. Suddenly there was a tremendous explosion which rocked the Sherman from side to side. The train disappeared in a violent cloud of red and yellow flame. An

---

[1] Most of the few radio messages Baum sent throughout the short life of his task force were relayed through Cub spotter planes to the division's listening posts.

[2] The only reason I can think of for this lack of air support is that Patton wanted as few people as possible outside his own Army to know of the Hammelburg mission.

ammunition car had been hit. When the flame vanished, all that was left of the train was four wheels neatly in place on the track.

The explosion was the signal for the battle to begin.

From all sides a heavy volume of bazooka and machine-gun fire hit the advancing Shermans and the following infantry. At first the enemy shooting was wild, surprised and uncoordinated. But after a few minutes it took shape and German machine gunners, obviously under experienced direction now, started to fire low and aim at the infantry platoon leaders.

Startled German Soldiers, some only half dressed and without their helmets, yet all armed, started to run down the cobbled, tree-lined road from the station, covered from the American fire by a bend in the road. There seemed to be scores of them.

When Baum realized the strength of the opposition which had suddenly appeared in the little town, he was surprised. He hadn't expected Gemünden to be a walkover in any shape or form, but he had not anticipated that the small town would be so strongly defended. Quick interrogation of one of the prisoners the infantry was already beginning to herd back soon enlightened him. As he recalled after the war:

> After further investigation, a prisoner told us that the region around Lohr and Gemünden was a marshaling yard for two German divisions and that one division had just unloaded in Gemünden. I believed it, as the Krauts were filtering all over the place.

He looked across at Stiller. Even his tough, taut narrow face was expressive with shock. Baum did not need to be clairvoyant to read what Major Stiller was thinking at this particular moment. *How the hell were three hundred men going to force a passage across the river against a whole German infantry division?*

Young Second Lieutenant Nutto, commanding the Shermans, felt absolutely naked, in spite of the armored walls of the medium tank, as he crawled toward the bridge behind the lead tank. He had been in combat long enough to know the fatal weaknesses of the Sherman. Whatever the wheels in the "head shed" (divisional headquarters) said to to the contrary, the tank's high silhouette, gently sloping glacis plate[3] and gasoline engine made it easy prey for anti-tank fire, whether from a cannon or a bazooka. One round close to the rear sprocket wheel was usually sufficient to set the Sherman afire, turning it into a blazing metal death trap.

Now he was in ideal bazooka country. Fifty yards ahead, the lead tank was advancing cautiously into the narrow curving street that ran down to the ancient four-span bridge. At any moment a Kraut Panzerfaust gunner could crack into action from one of the shattered windows of the houses which lined the street—and that would be that. The Sherman would be stopped dead, blocking the whole street and barring the way to the bridge which still seemed deceptively peaceful, though he knew now that somewhere on the other side lay strong German defenses.

He tried to forget the disturbing possibility and concentrated on the task at hand. Up front, Sutton's infantry crouched close to the walls on either side of the road, ready to race ahead once the tanks had dealt with any opposition. Nutto raised his head out of the turret and scanned his front anxiously. To his immediate front lay an ancient ruined castle on top of the hill. It looked to him an ideal place to place an artillery observer. Someone posted up there could see the whole valley below and far out up the road where Baum was waiting with the rest of the column. Nutto felt the castle would be soon worthy of a couple of rounds of high explosive. To the right of the bridge, on the other side of what looked like a drainage ditch or a small arm of the river, there lay a line of ancient half-timbered, white-painted houses with red roofs. They sat there in ominous silence with no sign of movement coming from them. But Nutto noted that none of the shutters on the houses were closed, as they probably would have been if their owners were present—they would have

---

[3]Glacis plate is the front armor of the tank. German tanks, such as the Panther, had the glacis plate so heavily armored and cast at such an angle that shells often bounced off it.

wanted their valuable glass panes protected. No, the row of houses would be due for a salvo if trouble started, he decided; they probably contained German infantry. At that moment, in fact, he had a decidedly unpleasant feeling that the whole far bank of the river was lined with tense German soldiers, waiting for some officer to give them the order to fire at this foolish little band of Yanks who had the temerity to attack *their* bridge.

Nutto was not to wait long before he found out how right he was. The leading Sherman was within fifty yards of the bridge when there was a sharp dry crack like that of a dry branch snapped underfoot in a summer forest. It was a sound that Nutto was coming to know well. A Kraut Panzerfaust!

Flame shot from one of the windows of the houses on this side of the bridge. A shower of angry red sparks followed. The next moment there was the hollow echoing sound of metal striking metal. The lead Sherman jolted to a sudden stop, a fresh, gleaming hole gouged in its side. Then the fun really started. Small arms crackled along the far side of the bridge like summer lighting.

Sutton ordered his men into action. They started to race for the bridge, firing from the hip as they went. Spandaus whirred into action, filling the morning air with high-velocity lead. A man stopped suddenly, threw his hands straight upward in a dramatic gesture and then pitched face forward onto the cobbles with a thud. Nutto felt sickened. More bazookamen joined the action. Another Sherman was hit. The infantry ran on. They were almost there now. Nutto bit his lower lip. They were going to make it after all! The volume of fire rose to a crescendo. It seemed to be coming from all sides now. Everywhere Nutto looked he could see the red and yellow flashes of small-arms fire.

Two of Sutton's infantry were on the bridge now. Behind them their platoon commander lay in the gutter wounded. They were pelting across, oblivious to the hail of lead coming their way. They were halfway across now. They seemed to bear charmed lives. Nothing was going to stop the two armored battalion doughs. A few more yards and they would be across. The vital, all-important bridge would be theirs.

And then suddenly and frighteningly the bridge seemed to leap into the air. There was a terrible dull roar. A great chunk of masonry flew into the air, followed by a violent ball of red and yellow flame. A cloud of smoke shot up, obscuring forever the two lone armored infantrymen, who had given their lives in vain.

Everything now was confusion. The Shermans milled around in the narrow street, assailed on all sides, while the infantry kneeled or crouched with their backs to the nearest wall, firing burst after burst against the windows of the houses opposite. Nutto realized the situation was quickly getting out of hand. They had lost the bridge and were getting themselves into a decidedly sticky situation here. Someone had better do something—and soon!

Hurriedly he and his driver reversed the medium tank in the direction of the waiting column now staring anxiously up the road where their last chance of getting to Hammelburg by the direct route had just gone up in smoke and flame.

Dismounting swiftly, he ran over to where Baum stood, map in hand next to a Sherman. A little out of breath and not very coherently, he reported the situation at the bridge, while Baum listened, a worried frown on his tough young face.

He had just finished when there was that familiar dry crack again. The next instant a bazooka round exploded a couple of yards away. Fragments hummed through the air all around them. Nutto felt a sharp stinging pain in his leg and to his great surprise found himself sprawled on the ground. Baum was wounded too—in the knee and right hand, touching the bone in both places.

Groggily Nutto was helped to his feet, and still in shock stared at the dark red blood trickling down the cloth of his torn pants. Baum, breathing hard with pain, looked at him; then at his leg. "You've had it," he exclaimed. "Better get into the half-track and lie down." Nutto was about to contradict him when the first wave of red angry pain hit him. He felt his eyes go misty with tears of agony and he knew he couldn't fight on. Grateful for their support, he allowed two doughs to take him back to the half-track.

Quickly Baum had his hand bound up by one of the two medics, who now had their work cut out looking after the thin but steady stream of wounded coming back from the bridge. Then he got down to considering his position. He had lost a bunch of infantry, including a platoon leader. Nutto was too wounded to fight and he had lost another three of his valuable Shermans, reducing his fire power considerably. But, most important of all, he had lost the valuable bridge across the Saale. What now?

While Stiller looked anxiously but silently over his shoulder, Baum ignored the throb in his leg and studied the map. There was an alternate route, running directly north from Gemünden up to Burgsinn and then on to Bad Brückenau where his map gave out. To the east of that narrow winding road lay Hammelburg—only a matter of miles away. But there was a catch. The River Sinn lay between the road and Hammelburg. *Where would he find a bridge intact?*

He bit his lip anxiously. What was he going to do? Up ahead the fight was still going on. Although he couldn't see it, German infantry had swarmed onto one of his Shermans in the narrow street and were trying to force open its hatches so that they could throw a grenade inside. Desperately, the sweating men inside swung their piece round and round trying to swat them off like some enraged primeval monster trapped by a group of primitive cave men.

Baum made a decision. One of the prisoners he had grilled previously had seemed to know the area fairly well. Now he stepped up to the man and through an interpreter began to grill him on the subject of a bridge across the Sinn. At first the man denied a bridge existed. But Baum grew tough. His wound hurt and the situation was desperate. He needed that information and—by God —he needed it quick!

The prisoner's eyes grew round with fear. He ran a

trembling hand up the side of his face and thrust it through his long lank hair. Finally he gave in. *"Ja, ja,"* he stuttered eagerly to the soldier doing the interpreting, *"es gibt eine Brücke in Burgsinn."*

Baum seized on the name even before the interpreter had translated.

"Burgsinn!" he exclaimed. Quickly he glanced at the map. The place—a small town—was six miles to the north. It would do. From there a small road seemed to lead to Hammelburg a few miles away.

Hurriedly he rapped out his orders. The men at the bridge were to disengage. The light tanks were to take up the lead again. The wounded were to be loaded in the half-tracks at once even if they hadn't been attended to yet. A radio message was to be flashed to divisional headquarters telling them of the marshaling yards at Gemünden and requesting an air strike.

In no time the column, waiting tensely at the side of the road in small groups of anxious men who smoked their cigarettes in tense, nervous puffs, was transformed once more into an experienced, trained military unit. Officers snapped orders. NCO's lumbered down the road, harassing their men. The GI's sprang into their vehicles. "Roll 'em!" someone shouted. Motors sprang to life. Great clouds of blue smoke shot out of the tank exhausts. The column started to move forward again.

Baum took up his usual position behind the tanks. Beside him in the command peep sat the scared, unkempt German prisoner, his eyes rolling with fear. With good reason. Baum was making sure that there should be no trickery on the man's part. And the latter knew better than to trifle; the ferocity in Baum's eyes was unmistakable.

Slowly the column began to grind its way up the steep hill that lead north to Burgsinn, leaving behind the smoldering ruins of three Shermans and the sprawled khaki-clad figures of their dead on the ancient cobbles of the street leading to the destroyed bridge. Gradually the sound of the firing died away and then stopped altogether.

Sunk in thought, Baum considered his situation. "The

bridge was the only one that would take us where we were going," he recalled later, "and the fight at Gemünden showed that bridges would come hard." Now the country-side would be seething with armed men. The Krauts wouldn't yet know that this was just a small raiding party. Perhaps they would figure it was a whole armored division moving in on them. It was obvious from the prisoners that the Germans were confused and scared. Nonetheless, his common sense told him that the enemy would not just let him barrel on like this. Somewhere at this very moment someone was probably giving the order which would set up a trap on the road ahead. It was a decidedly strong possibility.

Grimly Captain Abraham Baum, former ladies' blouse cutter and now commander of what was left of the three hundred men who had set out that morning and whose fates depended completely on the correctness of his deci-sions, began to stare at the thickly wooded sides of the road, as if each dark-green fir hid a potential ambush.

Shortly after the last of young Lieutenant Hoffner's men, who had covered the withdrawal, had left the alarmed, confused river town of Gemünden, a strange little group crept cautiously toward the ruined bridge. It was a three-man team from a combat propaganda outfit, headed by T/3 Ernst Langendorf, who spoke fluent Ger-man. It was an unusual outfit to find so far forward.

Langendorf had no idea that he was already some thirty-five miles behind the enemy lines. The confusion created by Baum's advance had made his team's journey over the rough country back roads a smooth little pleasure ride.

Langendorf, who was as earnest and conscientious as his first name, now went into action and carried out the orders given to him back at 4th Division HQ. He was to support Baum the best way he knew how. Seizing his microphone, Ernst launched into his usual propaganda spiel, which came easily now through long practice. *The war was over . . . why fight any longer . . . Hitler was crazy . . . he would soon be dead . . . the treatment given to German soldiers who surrendered was correct and in*

*accordance with the Geneva Convention . . . there'd be
food—including white bread . . . AND AMERICAN
CIGARETTES . . . LUCKY STRIKES AND CHESTER-
FIELDS . . .*

The mention of cigarettes did it!

Everywhere the gray-uniformed German soldiers
dropped their long rifles and raised their hands in surrender. Long streams of them, hands clasped behind their
necks, began to come out of the houses on both sides of
the river. Beaming with pride, Ernst started to count
them. There were three hundred of them in all!

He winked at his companions. Not a bad catch for
a ten-minute speech, his wink seemed to say. His companions grinned in return. But there was no time to waste.
Seizing his microphone once again, he told the waiting
men, whose faces dropped a little when they heard the
news, that he didn't have time to take them prisoner just
now; they would have to be patient till the next Ami outfit
arrived. There were a few grunts and murmurs of disap-
proval among the Wehrmacht men, who had been looking
forward to the *Ami Zigaretten* instead of the black mor-
khaka tobacco, flavored with something called "Virginia
Aroma," that they had smoked so long. But their years in
the Army had taught them obedience, so they complied.

Well satisfied with his morning's work, earnest Ernst
decided that he had earned his pay for that day. Turning
to his driver, he said, "Okay, let's turn back."

So the strange little outfit turned back and returned
the way it had come, without a shot having been fired
at them, unaware that they had just missed a bloody
little battle and that they had been miles behind enemy
lines all the time! Questioned on their return as to the
whereabouts of Task Force Baum, they shrugged their
shoulders and exclaimed, "We don't know."

Neither did anyone else. On that March morning, Task
Force Baum—after sending its first and only message of
the day: "SEND AIR TO ATTACK GEMÜNDEN
MARSHALING YARDS"—had disappeared completely
from human ken.

Chapter 9

1000 HRS
March 27

On the morning of March 27, General Patton moved his headquarters from France to Germany, transferring it to the picturesque hill town of Idar-Oberstein, some fifty miles west of the Rhine. The new headquarters was located in a former German infantry barracks, with Patton's own accommodation situated in the officers' club, still replete with unlooted regimental silver and china, all monogrammed with the regiment's number and heavily embossed with swastikas.

But General George S. Patton had no eyes for his new and rather luxurious surroundings that morning. He had other things to do, though he did find time to send an enormous carved eagle, which had adorned the former 107th German Infantry Regiment headquarters back to his old alma mater, West Point, as a gift. Three of his rampaging divisions seemed about to strike out for the same objective. The 80th and 76th Infantry Divisions and a task force from Hoge's old 9th Armored were all poised for an attack on the German town of Wiesbaden, and it looked to a worried Patton like the three outfits would soon be shooting each other up if he didn't do something about the mess quickly.

But while he went to work on the Wiesbaden mess, his mind was concerned with another problem. *Hammelburg and Task Force Baum!* Where the hell had they gotten to? Stiller hadn't yet reported and all that the 4th had heard from the force deep in the heart of enemy-held territory was the laconic message requesting air to attack Gemünden. In the pauses between sorting out the tricky situation with his three divisions, he repeatedly asked his staff officers to check the Hammelburg attack. But each time

the officer concerned checked, he found that neither
Abrams nor Hoge had anything to report. Baum and his
men had vanished completely! That day passed with no
news whatsoever coming in. That day Patton recorded in
his diary:

> We were very much disturbed because we could not get
> any information at all as to what had happened to the
> task force sent east from the 4th Armored Division.

General Patton had good reason to be alarmed. Finally
the Germans were wakening up to the danger in their
midst. After Task Force Baum was repulsed at Gemünden,
messages started to flash out from German headquarters
in Nuremberg to both civilian and military authorities.
The Nazi burgomaster of the little wine town of Hammelburg received a message at 10 o'clock on that Tuesday
morning to start evacuating the place. Burgomaster Cle-
ment needed no urging. Reaching as many people as possible by telephone, he warned the rest through the old
town crier, who hastened through the narrow streets, ringing his bell and croaking in his hoarse old wine-drinker's
voice:

> All noncombatants to leave the town at once! Take only
> immediate necessities with you! All noncombatants to . . .

The town's air raid siren began to wail thinly. Up in
the old church someone started to ring the bells. Everything was suddenly haste, confusion and fear. The Amis
were coming. They had to get away!

An eyewitness describes the scene thus:

> Chaos reigned in the narrow streets as the crowd of
> refugees hastened to the north and the east. Hurrying
> women, children and old men (there were few young ones
> left) rushed down the main escape route, their baggage
> loaded on little handcarts. There were also wagons, pulled
> by horses and slow plodding oxen, and laden with clothes,
> bedding, food and other household goods. Even pigs and
> chickens were loaded and taken away . . . There would
> have been a catastrophe if the jostling line of refugees had
> been spotted by fighter-bombers.

Soon the town was empty save for a few invalids and

stubborn old men and women, who refused to leave. Now it lay there in the sunny, sleepy little valley waiting for what was to come.

Up in the Hammelburg camp, General von Goeckel was also alarmed. He had heard the firing at Gemünden in the early hours of the morning, but had fallen asleep again when it had died away. Now, dressed in full uniform, pistol at his waist and helmet close at hand on his office desk, he got on the telephone to Nuremberg. He wanted news and advice.

He got both. And didn't like either very much. Headquarters informed him that an American armored spearhead had broken through at Aschaffenburg, had been repulsed at Gemünden and was heading north in his general direction on the other side of the River Sinn.

Again Goeckel asked that he be allowed to evacuate the camp. The clipped Prussian staff officer's voice at the other end snapped "No."

Goeckel raised his head and, with that gesture peculiar to him, fought for breath. Then he tried another tack. "Well, send me some troops then, in case the Amis come this way," he said.

"We have no reserve available to send you any men," the impersonal voice at the other end replied. "You'll have to make do with what you've got."

"But I've got only old men and . . ."

He didn't finish his sentence. The staff officer had put down the telephone.

Shaking his head at such impoliteness, Goeckel seized his helmet and hurried out of his office, ignoring the inquiring looks of both his own men and the American prisoners, who had also been alarmed by the sound of firing from the direction of Gemünden. Quickly he entered Colonel Hoppe's command post.

The former NCO, who had worked his way up to his present rank by virtue of his ability, was hollow-eyed and weary-looking this fine Tuesday morning. Goeckel told himself that he probably had been having trouble with his sharp-tongued virago of a wife again. How he could stand that woman, von Goeckel simply didn't know. But he had no time to worry about Frau Hoppe.

Swiftly the other officer rose to his feet and clicked his heels together. *"Morgen, Herr General,"* he barked with a trace of his old military smartness.

"Morgen, Hoppe," the general answered. "You've heard the news?"

The colonel nodded.

"So, and you know too that we're in a fine mess. Headquarters has just had the kindness to inform me that we will have to look after Hammelburg with our men." The tall general could not quite conceal the note of bitterness in his voice. "You with your twenty-man staff and your company of snipers. I with my three hundred cripples and congenital idiots. And against American tanks at that!"

Hoppe allowed himself a sympathetic grin, and said, "What are we going to do, sir?"

Goeckel shrugged expressively. "What we have always done all our lives, Hoppe—*obey orders.*"

Swiftly the two men got down to arranging the defense of the camp. Goeckel would assume responsibility for the prisoners and, in addition, muster what men he could spare to man his three strong points and form a defensive line. Hoppe would use his regular, combat-experienced snipers for a more aggressive role should the Americans appear. Together they could field about four hundred men, armed mostly with antiquated captured enemy rifles and machine guns, though Hoppe had a few light cannon at his disposal. It wasn't much to stop an enemy armored division, but old soldier von Goeckel, with nearly four decades of military experience behind him, was determined that the Americans wouldn't take Hammelburg without a fight.

Others were equally determined to meet this menace which had suddenly appeared in their midst on this fine Tuesday morning. At Bonnland, a small village a few miles south of Hammelburg camp, a Major Diefenbek had set his own little defensive operation in motion. Returning from Aschaffenburg a couple of days before, he had stopped at several farmhouses on the way back and told the locals to warn him if the enemy crossed the Main and passed their way. All they needed to do, he told them, was to get to the nearest telephone and say the words "Wasps' Nest."

This morning he had had three calls announcing "Wasps' nest" from farmers on the Gemünden-Burgsinn road. The tough combat engineer, who had had plenty of fighting experience on the Russian front, gathered his little force of engineers together, told them the news, and ordered them into their positions to await the Americans. Now Major Diefenbek sat in his command post, machine pistol close at hand, and calmly smoked a cigarette. He, too, was ready.

But there were more ferocious units than prison guards and combat engineers hurrying to contain the Americans. That morning three hundred hard-faced young men in camouflage uniforms were making a forced march toward Hammelburg from the direction of Gemünden. The going was tough across the rugged Franconian hills and the pace was hot, yet the sweating, blond young men did not falter. They were used to this sort of thing. They were Hitler's elite.

The young men were all officer-cadets of the hardest-fighting, most feared German outfit, the Waffen SS,[1] who wore their silver SS runic dog collars with an aggressive pride that had almost vanished from the rest of the German Army. All of them had had one year's front-line combat experience with an SS unit before being sent to officer-training school, where they had learned the courtesies of the officer's profession, *including dancing lessons and the formalities of exchanging cards when visiting* (this in the middle of the final disastrous year of war with the enemy within the boundaries of the Reich itself!). They had also learned, however, how to kill their enemy with half a

---

[1] The armed SS.

score deadly little tricks in the process of being toughened for their role as the elite leaders of the elite.[2]

Now, after being diverted from the march to the front at Gemünden, and angered by the deaths of several of their comrades in the bombing of the town which followed Baum's departure, they marched toward Hammelburg at a breakneck pace, blood in their eyes.

Slowly the German command began to recover from the shocked surprise of the American breakthrough that March morning. At Nuremberg, the hard-boiled German general staff officers, with years of professional training behind them, started to react. The few spotter planes still available were ordered into the sky to find the enemy's location and—more important—to report on his strength!

The German commanders knew their units were too weak and too scattered to oppose a full-scale American breakthrough, but they knew too that if the Amis were only an isolated group sent forward for God knows what purpose (and the reports now coming in from Gemünden seemed to indicate that they *were* an isolated group without any further support), then they could take them.

With that aim in mind, the German staff officers sent an urgent message to the local German commander at the little town of Meiningen, north of Hammelburg. It was a message that was to be decisive for the fate of Task Force Baum. It read simply:

Panzerjaeger nach Hammelburg—sofort.

Captain Lang was dying. Baum looked at Zeno's pale face and then at the young captain lying bloody in the gutter. "We can't take him with us?" he asked the medic. Zeno shook his head. The wounded officer's blood was beginning to flow across the cobbles.

Baum looked down at his fellow officer. Lang had come

---

[2] One nice little training habit was to make the cadet do numerous push-ups with an ivory-handled dagger (carried by every cadet as a sign of his rank) poised unsheathed under his naked chest. It was an ideal way to develop good arm muscles.

to the 4th as a replacement, and the 4th was an outfit that didn't particularly like replacements. But Baum had taken a liking to Lang. He was eager and brave and Baum had initiated his promotion to captain. Now he was going to have to leave him behind at the mercy of the Krauts. There was no other way out. They could take with them only those men who could still fight even though they were wounded. Baum shook his head.

"Okay," he said to Zeno. "See that hut?" He pointed to a wooden shack just off the road.

"Yessir."

"Well, put him and the others," (he indicated four other seriously wounded men) "into it and see you get a red cross flag on the roof so that the Krauts can see it."

Zeno got to work. Gently he and Demchak carried the officer and then the other four men into the hut, after which they spread one of the red and white flags they carried with them over the roof. Baum watched until they were finished, then without looking back, he gave the order for the column to move on. Getting into his jeep he ordered the driver to fall in behind the lead recon tanks. Slowly the column started to get underway, their tracks throwing up the fine dry dust, their exhausts choking the air with the putrid blue smoke of the gasoline engines.

Behind them Zeno and Demchak swung into their half-track and, shouting a few last words of encouragement to the men they were leaving behind, they too joined the column.

And then it happened! The lead tanks hadn't gone more than a mile when the air was torn apart by the vicious flight of an 88 mm. shell. Then another. "Incoming mail," someone cried.

"Gonna miss us," another GI yelled, unworried by the enemy fire. "Miles off." Then the words froze on his lips. The Germans weren't trying to hit the column. *They were shooting at the shack with the Red Cross flag on the roof!*

Everywhere in the half-tracks the GI's stared horrified at the hut with its five wounded, unsuspecting victims.

The first salvo missed. The second came closer. The

third hit it directly. With a roar the shack disappeared in a cloud of violent red and yellow smoke.

In his peep Baum groaned and struck his clenched fist into the palm of his other hand. *"Goddam,"* he cursed. *"Goddam . . ."*

The column rolled on.

That morning, sometime between nine and ten o'clock, the almost deserted cobbled street that led from the Hammelburg railway station began to echo hollowly with the clatter of heavy-tracked vehicles. Slowly, great camouflaged tanks appeared, one after another, their long, sinister, hooded cannon hidden under greenery, their decks laden with spare tracks (as extra protection) and long metallic cases of ammunition. They were Ferdinands, tank destroyers mounted on a Panther chassis, as fast as any Sherman, but with a 90-mm gun which could knock out the American tank frontally—where its armor was thickest—at 800 yards' range, whereas the Sherman, to do the same, would have to get within 200 yards and place a shell through the Ferdinand's periscope, measuring 2 by 8 inches!

Captain Koehl's detachment of TD's had arrived to do battle!

Chapter 10

1030 HRS March 27 | At almost exactly the same time that the feared German tank destroyers arrived at Hammelburg station, the Baum column was rumbling up a steep rise on their way to Burgsinn when the lead tank jammed on the brakes and came to a sudden halt.

A German staff car, accompanied by a motor cycle escort had suddenly appeared over the next hill. In the very moment that the lead tank spotted the Germans, the enemy driver spotted the Americans. He hit the brakes with his foot and the long camouflaged Horch slewed to a stop. A German officer grabbed his machine pistol and clicked home the magazine. He looked as if he were going to make a fight for it.

Too late!

The Americans reacted quicker. The gunner of the lead tank swished his 37-mm cannon warningly from left to right. The threatening gesture sufficed. The officer shrugged slightly and dropped his weapon. Slowly he raised his hands. He wanted to surrender. Reluctantly the remaining occupants of the German staff car followed suit.

The commander of the lead tank raised his head above the hatch and with his pistol in his hand told the Germans to "come on out—nice and slow like."

The Germans seemed to understand English, or perhaps the tone of the man's voice was indicative of what he wanted. They opened the door of the long great touring automobile and stepped out onto the dusty country road under the watchful eye of the American tank crew.

One of them, a tall man with a long leather coat, adorned with golden epaulettes, walked proudly past the tank toward Baum who had come up to see what the trouble was. As he approached the young American commander, he tugged at his gray gloves and spouted some voluble German.

"What do ya know?" someone cried as the man came closer and they could see the enemy's golden collar insignia. "It's a goddam Kraut general!"

"Who the hell are you?" Baum asked the leather-coated man roughly. The man tried to explain at length in rapid, excited German, but Baum cut him short. Time was being wasted.

"Get the son-of-a-bitch up in the half-track and let's get going," he ordered.

Without ceremony the surprised general and his staff were bundled into one of the empty half-tracks. The column moved on.

They crawled cautiously into Burgsinn. But there was no opposition there. And their frightened guide had been telling the truth. There was a bridge across the Sinn here—and it was intact. Joyously the point tank of the recon outfit passed the word back to Baum, who ordered the force to proceed. Hammelburg, according to the dust-covered yellow and black sign which decorated the bridge, was exactly nineteen kilometers away.

Pausing only to pick up a surprised civilian to guide them to the next village of Grafendorf, the column pressed on. As Baum remembers it: "We took off cross-country and went up a mountain valley till we hit the Saale valley." Now once again the Germans had lost Baum as he urged his force up steep, heavily wooded inclines in the hills that surrounded Grafendorf.

Ignorant of the fact that his advance was causing consternation as far away as Berlin (Berlin Radio had already broadcast that the defenders of Gemünden had "knocked out fifteen tanks of an enemy armored spearhead"), Baum plunged down the steep road into Grafendorf shortly before noon. Here he liberated a Russian POW and set free several hundred Russians to whom he gave the two hundred German prisoners he had already collected.

Although the wildly enthusiastic, half-starved Russians

assured him that they would arm themselves and continue guerrilla warfare in the woods until the Americans arrived in strength, Baum felt that most of them were most interested in getting drunk and filling their bellies—for which he could not blame them.

As the column began to roll again, the Russians started to break into stores and warehouses all over Grafendorf. A wild orgy of drinking and looting commenced and Sergeant Donald Yoerck caught one fleeting glance of a wildly screaming Russian, loaded to the gills with looted schnaps, chasing a guard into the woods with a gleaming naked bayonet, before his Sherman clattered over the rise that led out of the place.

As Captain Baum remembers it, the task force "crossed at Grafendorf and followed the Saale and the railroad line to Weickersgruben." Now they were within five miles of their goal and free of attack. It was exactly 1400 hours. Again Baum's hopes began to rise. They might pull it off after all. Even Stiller's mood seemed to have picked up. Perhaps the Russians' elation at being freed might have helped; Baum did not know. Stiller gave little away. Baum grinned at him and the older man's tough, leathery face cracked into a slow smile.

But not for long.

The column stopped so suddenly that Baum was nearly flung against the windshield of the tight little command peep.

"What the hell—" he began angrily, then his voice trailed away. He could *hear* the reason his lead tank had stopped and caused the driver of his own peep to hit the brakes so abruptly.

There was a plane circling around above them!

Swiftly he vaulted out of the peep. Grabbing the glasses hanging around his neck, he focused them furiously. It was a German spotter plane. A Fieseler Storch, he thought. And it had spotted them.

The young officer realized at once the vital importance of not letting the Kraut plane get away with the information. "Knock the bastard down—fire!" he yelled desperately.

The urgency conveyed by his order was contagious. Everywhere the long line of armored vehicles crackled into violent life, sending a stream of lead skyward. As Baum remembers: "Even the wounded in the half-tracks manned the machine guns in the vehicles. I passed up and down the column and saw them on the guns."

In spite of the heavy small-arms fire, the tiny German spotter plane came down for another look. Baum could see the black and white crosses underneath its wings quite plainly. Furiously the machine guns chattered, with the sweating gunners hanging onto their violently trembling 50-calibers as if their very lives depended upon it. But to no avail. All their bullets went wide. Finally, with one last contemptuous waggle of its wings, the little monoplane turned and flew northward. Within seconds it was just a speck on the horizon. In a minute it had disappeared altogether.

For one long angry moment, while the echo of the firing still died away in the surrounding hills, Baum stood alone on the road and stared at the disappearing plane. Around him the men at the blue-smoking guns, whose barrels were glowing a dull red, gazed at him in anxious silence. They knew exactly what their young commander was thinking at that particular instant. The Krauts had spotted them, but what was worse, the little plane would report their exact numbers. Now the German command would know they were not dealing with an armored division (as some of their POW's had told them was their belief) but with an isolated handful of tanks and infantry.

Then Baum turned and walked slowly back to his command peep in thoughtful silence. The column moved on.

A little while later the column stopped again. This time Baum knew for sure that the German plane had already made its report to its headquarters. As he remembers:
When we stopped, I heard vehicles moving. They were not any of ours. I oriented myself and decided which way to attack this town where the POW camp was located and

also figured out exactly where the American prisoners were. We left Weickersgruben . . . headed northeast and ran into German tanks near the next village, Ober,[1] a mile and a half from Hammelburg.

Task Force Baum had run head-on into Captain Koehl's detachment of tank destroyers!

At first Koehl had not been sure from which direction the Americans would come, if they were to come this way at all. Leaving Hammelburg just after ten o'clock that morning, he had disposed his great lumbering Ferdinands along the Fulda road to the north of the little Franconian wine town. But shortly afterward he had changed his mind and had led them back through the town to take up positions near the hamlet of Thulba, from whence his 90-mm.s could dominate the whole southern section of Hammelburg, besides covering the main Fulda-Würzburg highway which the enemy would have to cross to get to the POW camp (though naturally, Captain Koehl did not know at that time that this was the Americans' objective).

Once there, the young *Hauptmann* went to work speedily, consolidating his positions, putting into practice all that precious experience he had gained from years of fighting the Russian T-34 and monstrous Stalin tanks in the East.

Positioning his TD's at intervals all along the high ground, carefully selecting each individual site himself, he covered his valuable vehicles with small groups of infantry armed with automatic weapons, so that they would not be vunerable to infantry assault. Once they were in position, he went from Ferdinand to Ferdinand, ensuring that each one was camouflaged to the best of its ability and that each crew knew the distances and location of each feature of terrain of any importance within range. Satisfied that he had arranged his trap to the best of his ability, he ordered that no one was now to leave his position in any circumstances. "If you feel the call of nature, forget it," he told his men with a grin, "or do it in your pants." By two o'clock, when the first American tank hove cautiously

---

[1]He meant Obereschenbach.

into sight, *Hauptmann* Koehl, veteran of many a desperate action in the East, was ready and waiting to do battle with his American opponents.

An eyewitness (one of the few townsfolk who did not flee) recounts the start of the action:

> About two hours later [that afternoon] the first enemy tank appeared and began to crawl forward very slowly and cautiously. One by one six tanks came into sight, followed shortly afterward by armored personnel carriers. There must have been forty vehicles in all. Now they began to move down the road to Saaleck.

Koehl had seen them too. From his well-camouflaged positions on the hill, he noted mechanically that the enemy tanks appeared to be mainly Shermans and a smaller, lighter tank which he could not identify. He nodded to himself. He could handle them all right. With his binoculars he swept the line of half-tracks, filled—it appeared—with infantry. Then he cursed. Sergeant Graham's self-propelled guns, with their long 105-mm cannon had appeared in his vision. *"Scheisse!"* he cursed. They were a different proposition altogether.

Lowering his glasses, he raised his helmet and wiped his brow free of sweat in spite of the fact that the day wasn't warm. He smiled at himself. It was probably the sight of those Ami SP's which had made him break out in perspiration. Then his smile vanished. There was work to be done. Pulling down his helmet, he clambered onto his own TD. The crew was tense and a little nervous, he could see that. But the gunner was crouched over his piece, eye glued to the rubber eyepiece. He flung a glance to left and right. Although none of his crews were to be seen outside of their vehicles, he could somehow sense that they, too, were crouched in their steel boxes, waiting tense and nervous like his own men.

The Americans were getting closer. Now he could see the white stars painted on their metal sides quite plainly. He nudged his gunner. The man took his eye away from the sight and stared up at him almost angrily. "Take the Sherman at ten o'clock," Koehl whispered, as if the Americans could hear him at this distance. The man grunted something unintelligible, but did as he was told. The great long gun, weighed down by the muzzle brake at the end, swung round slowly and menacingly until it was pointing at the leading tank.

The Americans were less than three hundred yards away now. They were just crawling along and it surprised Koehl a little that they had not yet spotted him. The German captain flung a look at the town of Hammelburg down below in the valley, with its fine old late Gothic steeple reaching up above the huddle of medieval houses. He had fought a lot of battles since he had joined the Army. He had experienced the great victories of the early war years and the bitter defeats of the frozen, wintry Russian steppe. Now he was to do battle in the heart of his homeland. Perhaps here, just outside this sleepy Franconian wine town that had graced this valley since the days of the great Frankish king Charlemagne, he was fated to die. But, he told himself with a sudden clenching of his teeth and a hardening of his jaw, there were worse places to die than defending your own homeland.

The next minute he gave his command and the word came out at a roar, as if he were commanding a battalion of Ferdinands and these were the old days of the great victories—instead of a detachment, manned by callow 17-year-old boys and weary old men, the last scrapings of the barrel in the year of defeat. "FIRE!"

The gunner pulled his lever.

There was a tremendous roar. The tank shuddered violently. The breech came roaring back and the gleaming, hot yellow cartridge fell tumbling to the metal floor. Automatically Koehl opened his mouth of long practice. The acrid, cordite-laden hot blast slapped him flat in the face like a flabby fist. Equally automatically, he noted that the gunner was still inexperienced enough to keep his mouth closed. *He* would not keep his eardrums intact very long if he stayed in the artillery, he told himself, and reached for his glasses.

The result was disappointing. When the smoke had cleared, he saw that the first round had fallen too short.

"Scheisse!" he cursed. *"Verfluchte Scheisse!"* How were they training gunners these days?

He gave the young gunner a hard dig in the ribs and the man fired again. Now all his TD's joined in, firing from their camouflaged positions. With absolute finality the still afternoon was suddenly torn apart by shellfire. The battle for Hammelburg had begun!

Chapter 11

As the crash and crack of Koehl's great
TD cannon hit the camp on the hill, Colonel
Goode and the Jesuit priest, Father Cava-
naugh, rushed to the high wire fence that surrounded the
Oflag. Outside complete confusion reigned!

Goeckel's elderly militiamen were scrambling through
the fields outside, scattering the startled sheep as they ran
to take up their prepared positions along the crest of the
hill. Goode noted that there must be a couple of platoons
of them in all. Meanwhile, what looked like a company
of Germans were running heavily down the road to their
foxholes, which lay astride each side of it. With a professional eye the American infantry colonel noticed that the
enemy positions were well sited and, as always with the
Germans, their foxholes were dug deep and carefully
camouflaged. It seemed, Goode reflected that one could
never teach GI's to dig a hole deep enough; they were
just too goddam lazy.

Then his eye fell on the two 40-mm rapid-fire Bofors
cannon on the side of the road to Hammelburg. He
stroked his long nose thoughtfully. They'd give an attacker
a lot of trouble. Goeckel's infantry were poor quality, but
those damned cannon would be a hard nut to crack. Pray
God that Goeckel's men defending them would run when
the fireworks began.

Suddenly his attention was diverted from the German
guns.

Somewhere beyond, the volume of fire started to grow
dramatically. Goode turned to the priest, a dark-haired
man in his late thirties, and remarked, "That's the way
a tank battle starts, Padre. I've heard enough of them

to know. General Patton's boys are getting closer and the Germans are going to move us out of here."

Father Cavanaugh nodded his understanding and Goode quickly explained that twice that day he had stalled Goeckel in the hope of holding off any move before the American troops arrived.

"Well, let's hope they get here soon," the priest said and then, turning, walked back to his barracks.

The compound was now alive with excited men. A mass of them headed for the kitchen to break into their precious supplies for one last glorious bash before the relief force arrived. Others went over to Cavanaugh's barracks where he was hearing confessions prior to celebrating mass. Goode was just about to discuss the situation with Waters when the English-speaking German liaison officer Captain Fuchs told him that General von Goeckel wished to speak to him urgently.

Goeckel was waiting for him in his—Goode's—office. With him were several other American officers and the Serbian senior officer—a general—and his staff. Goode saluted and sat down on a hard chair; the conference could begin.

Goeckel's face was serious. Five minutes before, he had seen the first American tanks—a light tank which he could not identify—crawl into view across the ranges two kilometers southeast of the camp. It was clear to him that Oflag VII was their objective and that soon the thing he dreaded most was going to happen: he would have to defend the camp with his three hundred idiots and old men.

Quickly he sketched in the situation. "An American task force has broken through the German front and appears about to attack the camp . . ."

Goode opened his mouth as if he wanted to say something, but Goeckel did not give him a chance.

With unaccustomed rapidity of speech (owing to his lack of breath he normally spoke unusually slowly with long pauses between groups of words), he plunged on. "We shall defend ourselves naturally, as well as we can. Now it is possible that I shall be *your* prisoner this evening, but for the time being you are still *my* prisoners, for whom I am responsible."

He paused briefly for breath and noted the happiness which was beginning to creep into his prisoners' eyes, as they realized the full implication of his words.

"Please," he went on, "see that your people go into the cellars and the air raid trenches and ensure that they stay there during the course of any action. Tell them to keep quiet and remain neutral during any fighting. It would be foolish, gentlemen, to do anything stupid at this late stage of the game, which might have serious consequences."

He explained that soon he would have the camp's air raid siren sounded and this would be the signal for the prisoners to go to their cellars and air raid shelters, which had been dug out between the individual huts. The Serbian general and Goode nodded their agreement.

Then Goeckel gave them his final words.

"Gentlemen," he said softly and slowly so that every word registered, "I would ask you to be patient for another few hours, then I have given orders that at the least sign of any trouble on the part of the prisoners, *my men are to fire into the compound with their machine guns!* You understand?"

Goode walked away from the meeting, with the blasts of the camp siren indicating that Goeckel was already putting his plan into operation. His mind was full of mixed emotions. On the one hand he was filled with a feeling of tremendous joy that soon he might be freed after being a prisoner so long; he was prepared to do anything to speed that long-awaited release. On the other hand, the scene was ripe for a massacre if one of Goeckel's morons panicked and started firing into the camp. The others would soon follow him. As Goode forced his way through the running, laughing kriegies, some of whom waved huge sandwiches of spam and German bread at him, the tough old infantry colonel felt a cold finger of fear trace its way down his spine at the thought that all these happy young men were his responsibility. He must keep them under control! *He must!* What had Goeckel said? *"My men are to fire into the compound with their machine guns . . ."*

Captain Baum had reacted quickly when the first bursts from Koehl's TD's had landed short in the meadow before him. The tremendous noise of their explosion and the great showers of earth and stone which flew into the sky told him straightaway that he was up against heavy cannon. Swiftly he got on the radio to Sergeant Graham with his three self-propelled 105's. "Get up onto that knoll at two o'clock and engage the enemy!" he roared into the mouthpiece, trying to drown out the noise of battle which was growing louder by the minute.

"Yes, sir," Graham answered. "Will do."

At top speed the three SP's lumbered forward to the knoll, which was bare of trees so that they could easily give—and *take*—fire, and prepared to go into action.

Meanwhile the remaining Shermans opened up, giving covering fire to the light tanks and half-tracks which were trying to slip away up the steep road which led to the camp itself. Baum had ordered them to break off the action so that his whole force, especially his light-skinned vehicles which would be sitting ducks for the German heavy guns anyway, wouldn't get bogged down in the valley.

Now, with his force disposed the best he could, Baum watched the course of the action with horrified fascination. Up front, near what appeared to be a small wayside chapel, his leading Sherman was taking on the much superior German armor at less than 600 yards' range. He could see how the stationary tank shuddered slightly every time it fired. Through the smoke, dust and spurt of flame he watched the trace of the shot through his binoculars. It curved slowly and slightly upward at first, and then seemed to plunge swiftly with ever increasing speed at its target. Once there was the unmistakable glow of steel striking steel. Beside him Stiller yelled something enthusiastic, but Baum couldn't hear what he said through the din. "Fire again," he himself cried, carried away by the excitement of the battle. "Get the bastards!"

But the bastards weren't to be got. Their armor was proving too tough for the Shermans. Once Baum even saw a Sherman's shell zoom off at an angle after failing to penetrate the enemy TD's glacis plate. Now the 105's cracked into action with a hellish roar. Pfc. Herbert Reynolds, the first gunner to get on target, sent a salvo of smoke shells in the Germans' direction. "Damn fine thinking," Stiller yelled. The smoke would blind the superior German armor.

But it didn't.

The next moment, even as Stiller spoke, flame and smoke sprang from one of the TD's great banging gun. In an instant all was chaos in the leading Sherman. There was a great clang of steel on its turret, followed by a dull explosion. Shock waves swept through the interior, leaving the crew dazed, breathless and bleeding from both ears and nose.

The tank's interior was a bloody shambles. The solid armor-piercing shell had penetrated the front of the turret just near the gunner. Tracing a path along the metal like a hot knife in butter, it had swung across the turret, still glowing a vicious red, wrecking everything in its path. Miraculously it did not hit one of the crew save the gunner, whose shining red blood spurted out to splash the walls of the vehicle.

But now another danger presented itself. On the littered, jumbled floor of the Sherman countless small, greedy tongues of yellow flame were licking menacingly near the main ammunition storage rack. For a moment the shocked crew stared at them in bemused, paralyzed bewilderment. Then someone cried, "Let's get the hell out of here! *NOW!*" Faces blackened, eyes blinded by the smoke and the acrid fumes leaking from the batteries, the crew scrambled desperately out of their vehicle and pelted for safety, followed by the frustrated chatter of a German Spandau, angry at being tricked out of its tribute of blood.

Another Sherman was hit, came to an abrupt stop and began to burn, as they always did. It seemed to the angry 4th Armored crews that the smallest piece of metal striking the Sherman anywhere on its superstructure would turn it into a blazing mess in a matter of minutes. It was a standing grievance with the Sherman crews, but at that moment they had no time to consider the pros and cons of the Allies' most frequently used tank. The German fire was growing more intense by the second.

Tank shells and machine-gun fire poured into the column. A flat crack. A double boom of the explosion. The sound of ripping canvas, and the next moment there was the great hollow ring of metal striking metal, or a great brown hole appeared in the meadow as if dug out by some gigantic mole.

Another Sherman was hit and skidded to a stop. Flames began to crackle up from the region of its engine. But there was no movement from the stricken vehicle. Inside, the dead or stunned crew were slowly roasted as the tank turned a dull-glowing hot red.

Sickened, Baum jerked his head away. "Goddamnit," he cursed to himself, the lousy Kraut TD's were going to knock him out even before he got to the camp.

But the Germans were suffering losses too. Gunner Reynolds in the leading 105 had changed over to high explosive and was plastering a number of German trucks with schoolboyish glee. His first rounds were unsuccessful, but then suddenly he struck lucky. There was a tremendous roar as his next shot hit the leading truck. It was followed by another and another as the other trucks disintegrated, strewing bits and pieces of debris over a couple of hundred yards. The trucks had been loaded with ammunition for the German TD's.

Now the Germans began to take casualties. Down at the edge of the town German wounded were being dragged into the cellars, where the civilians who had refused to leave the place were sheltering. A couple of the men were badly wounded and it was clear that they had to have medical attention at once. But no one wanted to risk taking them to the nearest aid station. Suddenly, burly big-bosomed Frau Huber, wife of the local brewer, got to her feet. Looking at the few men, her eyes filled with disgust, she snorted above the noise, "I'll take them!"

Quickly a horse, an ancient flea-bitten animal whose ribs could be counted individually, was saddled to the brewer's cart and the wounded loaded. Taking the reins, the heavy-bosomed brewer's wife urged the horse up the road, seemingly oblivious to the shells falling around her everywhere.

It took her five minutes to reach the bridge across the River Saale. Here a group of wild-eyed German infantry ran out of their positions to meet her, yelling, "You can't go any further, woman! The bridge is under direct enemy artillery fire!"

Frau Huber looked at the teen-aged soldiers in disgust. Thrusting out her majestic bosom, she was just about to give these smooth-faced boys a piece of her mind when an American shell dropped out of the sky a few yards away. The boys took cover at once. But the ancient nag, which had never moved faster than a walk in all its working life, broke suddenly into a gallop. With a sweating Frau Hubner holding onto the reins for all she was worth, the cart shot across the bridge, down the street and into the town, with the horse going as if it were trying to win the Berlin Derby.[1]

The tank battle had been going on for almost two hours. Baum's Shermans were nearly all damaged or knocked out of action. Behind him on the road to Hammelburg, his light-skinned vehicles had also suffered some losses. As Baum remembers it:

> The Kraut tanks knocked out five of my half-tracks and three peeps—one of them was a medic peep. One of the half-tracks that was hit was filled with gasoline and the other carried 105–mm. ammunition.

The steep hill road that led to the camp was lined by now with a confused mess of burning half-tracks, from which the oily, dull, red flames crackled and roared with an intensity that threatened to continue until well after dark.

---

[1] And it didn't stop until it reached the aid station in the local hospital, where its breath finally gave out. A few days later the horse died; the strain of this one hectic gallop of its life seemingly too much for it.

Staring at the burning vehicles and realizing that he was getting weaker by the moment, young Captain Baum decided that the time had come to break off the action.

His crews had been taking a beating for long enough. Locked in their fume-filled iron boxes, they had answered the call of nature by urinating into one of the empty shell cases. (At five dollars a time it was one of the most expensive ways of relieving the bowels known to man, but it was cheaper than having your head blown off by a German 90-mm.) But that was all the personal attention they had allowed themselves. Everything else was concentrated on the little piece of ground they could see through the scaled glass of their periscopes and gun sights.

Baum made his decision. Grabbing his mike, he started to rap out orders.

Graham's 105's poured smoke down on the German positions. The rearmost tanks started to reverse with a noisy crash of gears and to back up the way they had come, while the Shermans to the front intensified their fire to cover the retreat.

Up on the hill Captain Koehl spotted the American intention immediately. Lowering his binoculars, he too rapped out a stream of orders. "Up your range! Try to get that Sherman to the rear. Gunner, change your target to Sherman at four o'clock." Urgently he tried to get his crews to increase their rate of fire. The Amis were running away. They mustn't be given a chance. Now was the time to finish them off altogether. Now, in the confusion and lack of coordination that always characterized a retreat.

But the TD crews responded halfheartedly. They were glad that the Amis were running away and the danger was over for the time being. Koehl did not need to be a clairvoyant to read their minds. They'd had enough. He sighed and gave in. Licking his lips drily, he surveyed the battlefield. Not bad at all for inexperienced troops—ten enemy armored vehicles knocked out at the cost of his munition trucks and one TD put out of action. Not bad at all.

Relaxing at last, the German captain felt the energy

drain out of him, almost as if a faucet had been opened and let it out. He let his shoulders slump and, taking off his helmet, wiped his sweating brow.

Below in the valley the last of the Shermans was reversing along the littered, shell-cratered road to Hammelburg, chased by the last ill-aimed shots of his exhausted crews. The field of battle was his. He had won for the time being. Taking a crumpled pack of evil-smelling cigarettes out of his pocket, he lit one and exhaled a satisfied stream of blue smoke while his crew sprawled out around him. Relaxed now, the tension gone, they chattered away excitedly about their success. Koehl looked at them, feeling old—very old. So they had won, but, he realized abruptly with a cold sensation akin to fear, only for the time being. They would meet the Amis again. Of that he was sure.

Chapter 12

1630 HRS March 27 Back in the noisy confusion of the excited camp, Father Cavanaugh was celebrating mass in his hut, dressed in the precious vestments of his calling, which he had managed to keep hidden from the Germans for so long.

The last stragglers dashed into the hut as the sound of the sirens died away and the noise of the battle grew louder. They included a Lieutenant Smolka, who wasn't a Catholic, but who had dashed into Cavanaugh's hut because it was the nearest. In spite of the first shells which were beginning to fall outside on the German Army compound, he watched the proceedings with interest.

"Since no more can get here," Cavanaugh said, his face pale with pent-up emotion, "I will start Mass immediately and give you General Absolution before Holy Communion."

Hastily he turned and began to say the Latin prayers before the "altar," which usually served as a mess table. For once he was glad he could turn his back on the huddled congregation; he was badly frightened and didn't want to show it to these men, who depended upon him so much.

The service began.

Just as he reached the Gospel, a shell shrieked across the camp with a hellish howl and landed with a huge crash a few yards away. As one man, the congregation dropped to the floor. His good precepts forgotten, Cavanaugh joined them.

After a moment's consideration, the Jesuit gritted his teeth and decided to come out of his distinctly unusual hiding place—underneath the altar. He didn't like it one bit, but he knew he had to set an example.

Trying to control his voice, he told his congregation to remain kneeling and try to keep calm. "If anything happens, just stretch out on the floor. I'll give you General Absolution now." As he raised his hand to bless them, he saw to his consternation that his fingers were shaking violently.

Making the sign of the cross over the kneeling men, he said, "Men, be calm. I'm going to shorten this Mass as much as possible so that everyone may get to Holy Communion."

He began reading the *Hanc Igitur* prayer: "Graciously accept O Lord this offering of our subjection to you. Give us peace today. Save us from eternal damnation and number us in the flock of your chosen ones, through Christ our Lord."

Smolka watched the simple ceremony, completely oblivious to the shells outside. He was utterly fascinated by the dark-haired priest carrying out this age-old ceremony in spite of the mayhem and murder going on outside. Suddenly the thin rays of the late afternoon sun penetrated the window. They illuminated the body of the priest in a thin, dusty yellow light. At that moment the young non-Catholic officer thought the priest "looked as if he were a God."

> "I kept pushing the task force over the ridge onto the high ground where two companies of Kraut infantry were dug in. It took us two and a half hours to clean it up so the infantry and tanks could move in."

Thus Baum recollects the action which led to the assault on the camp.

General von Goeckel remembers the preliminary action much differently. After inspecting his compound where the prisoners in their foxholes "saluted with an enthusiasm they had never shown before," he had his lunch brought as always by his wife, who did not seem to notice the shellfire.[1] Then he returned to his command post. From

---

[1] In spite of the "battle," good *hausfrau* von Goeckel believed her husband "couldn't manage without a solid midday meal."

there he watched the progress of the attack of which he writes:

It was no advertisement for the U.S. Army. The tanks approached in open formation to within 800 meters of the camp where my men opened fire with their machine guns. The tanks stopped and started to return the fire with their own machine guns, and at the same time began to fire shells into the Serbian compound. One of the main targets seemed to be the camp's water tower. Then they hit a large wooden hut, which housed the Serbs' hobby room. It went up in flames. That was about seventeen hundred hours . . . I expected then they would overrun the wire fence guarding the camp. After all there was nothing to stop them. But to my surprise they did nothing. Instead they remained at 500 to 800 meters' distance, firing their cannon from time to time.

Today it is very hard to get at the truth of the matter. No one seems to be able to tell the inquirer what happened between 1700 hours and darkness—at about 2000 hours—save that Baum's tanks, remaining outside the camp, fired continually into the Serbian compound. But in that period the man whom Baum had come—unknowingly—to rescue nearly lost his life.

Waters had been watching the tank action with some professional interest and he too wondered why the tankers were taking so long to penetrate the camp. He noted too that most of the shells were landing in the Serbian compound and wondered what the Serbs must be thinking at this moment of their American allies. He did not have time to consider very long.

Goode had been asked by the general in charge of the Serbs if he would go outside the camp and ask the Americans to stop the firing. Goode agreed to do so and asked Waters if he would accompany him. Waters readily agreed.[2]

---

[2] The few American writers on the Hammelburg affair maintain that General von Goeckel in a state of panic asked the Americans to stop firing. Goeckel himself states that the white flag mission was carried out without his knowledge as he was already in his command post behind the camp. According to him, it was probably

A white flag was quickly improvised and a large American Stars and Stripes appeared from somewhere—no one later knew quite from where. Then, together with two officers who bore the flags, Goode, Waters and the German liaison officer Captain Fuchs stepped out of the door, braving the odd shell that kept landing in the American compound with persistent and frightening regularity. At a brisk pace they set off toward the American tanks.

Outside, the scene was chaotic. Illuminated by the dancing, garish flames of the burning barracks, Waters could see the middle-aged German guards running back and forth, firing desperately at the American tanks, which were simply too much for them. To Waters it appeared as if the panic-stricken Germans were ready to drop their weapons and flee at any moment.

Steadily the little group advanced toward the tanks. The Shermans were in a hull-down position, from which they presented the smallest possible target, yet every time they fired, their high black silhouettes sprang into view. Once or twice a shell dropped short, and one of the officers carrying the flag cursed. Waters smiled in spite of the close call. Wouldn't it be damned ironic, he thought, if he were hit by one of his own people. But at that moment he had no thoughts of death. His mind was filled with the knowledge that in a matter of moments the long imprisonment would be over. He would be a free man again and back with his own people. He quickened his pace, the others instinctively following suit. The noise of the battle grew louder and louder.

Suddenly a dim figure loomed up in the darkness. Waters was the first to spot him. The man seemed to be dressed in some sort of camouflaged suit. Perhaps he was a paratrooper, Waters thought. He knew that American paratroopers wore camouflage. One of the rescue team is the thought that shot through his head.

"Amerikanisch?" he called hesitantly.

The figure in the dark hesitated one brief moment.

Waters waited expectantly.

Captain Fuchs who gave the order on his own. Knowing General von Goeckel, I am inclined to believe the German.

Then the man poked his rifle through the wooden fence which separated him from the little party. Before a startled and much alarmed Captain Fuchs could stop him, he cursed something in German and fired.

The slug hit Waters at fifteen yards' range. With a cry of pain, he felt the slug penetrate his body. He was flung back into the ditch at the side of the path, feeling as if he had been "hit with a baseball bat."[3]

The unknown German soldier was a determined man. While the party had still not recovered from its shock, he vaulted the wooden fence and backed a frightened Captain Fuchs at rifle point against a shed wall. Unable to do anything, the party looked on horrified while the soldier screamed that he was going to shoot the German captain there and then.

His eyes bulging with fear, Fuchs protested excitedly that they were parliamentaries. They were on their way to halt the American fire. They were under orders from higher authority. This wasn't a surrender. This was just a truce . . .

For several harrowing moments Fuchs talked urgently and rapidly at the glowering unknown soldier until finally the latter grunted sourly and lowered his rifle which was aimed at the German captain's belly.

Fuchs gave an audible sigh of relief and wiped the sweat off his brow with the back of a trembling hand,[4] while a half-conscious Waters sprawled in a ditch thought to himself angrily, Goddam it, you've ruined my hunting and fishing now!

Hurriedly Fuchs got hold of a blanket from somewhere and, their mission now forgotten, the little party began to carry the grievously wounded, profusely bleeding Colonel,

---

[3] In spite of the evidence to the contrary, General von Goeckel still believes that Waters' unknown assailant could have been an American soldier. The camouflaged suit could indicate, however, that the soldier was one of Hoppe's snipers as Goeckel's guards would be unlikely to possess such front-line equipment.

[4] Fuchs was to survive his narrow escape by only a matter of days. Escorting a group of POW's into the interior of the Reich after the abortive raid, he was killed in an Allied bombing raid as were many of his charges.

who had been shot through the upper thigh, back to the camp.

The man for whom the whole effort had been staged, for whom Baum's men had battled their way through sixty miles of enemy territory in the last twenty four hours, now lay bleeding profusely, trussed up in a gray German Army blanket like some stricken, dying animal . . .

It was now dark.

Two and a half hours had passed since the task force had made the first cautious approach to the camp and begun their artillery barrage. Now, through his binoculars, Baum, standing next to an impatient Stiller, could see the fires burning everywhere in the compound. He noted too that the volume of enemy small-arms fire was growing steadily less. Lowering the glasses, the young captain decided it was time that he launched his all-out attack. Time was getting on.

Seizing his mike, he rapped out a series of orders. The infantry was to rush the compound supported by the few remaining Shermans, while to the rear Sergeant Graham's two remaining 105's were to give covering fire. It was to be a do-or-die operation; a frontal assault with no time for the niceties of a carefully planned tactical flank operation.

Grimly the armored infantrymen of the 10th started the slow climb up the hill. They clung so close to the rear of the Shermans, lumbering forward in first gear that they could feel the hot fumes of the tanks' exhausts in their begrimed, unshaven faces. But that didn't matter—even if one or two of them actually got burned; they were darned grateful for the protection the tanks offered.

As they got closer to the crest and the German defense line, the volume of small-arms fire increased again, and the advancing GI's could see from the red line that ran and jumped erratically along the crest that not all the Krauts had yet bugged out; there were still some left who were prepared to fight it out. The tanks began to move faster. The infantry hurried to catch up with them and not lose that valuable protection.

To their rear Sergeant Graham gave his orders. Ammo

was running low, but this was the most vital phase of the whole operation and he knew he couldn't let the infantry doughs down. He snapped the command: "FIRE!"

The 105's cracked into action with a roar. There was a great hush and the heavy shells whizzed toward the German positions. The infantry pushed on. Now they were beginning to take casualties. Men were dropping everywhere on the slope. Here and there a man cried out loud for a medic in shocked angry bewilderment that this terrible hurt had been done to him. But there were others who lay crumpled and still, oblivious to the murder and mayhem around them in the dark fields pitted now with great brown holes. They would never move again. They were dead,[5] dying to save a man they were fated never to see.

"The hottest spot for the infantry guys," Sergeant Graham remembers, "was around the stockade. We were receiving machine-gun and sniper fire from there. We knocked out all we could. When we stormed the stockade I saw one of our men get hit by machine-gun fire, fall down and raise up and fire at the gun that hit him. He was on foot and got hit quite bad. He got to his knees and fired until they mowed him down."

Captain Baum, who was also worried about casualties, recalls: "That was typical of the whole operation. And my medics were operating the best they ever did. When evacuating wounded, they would take Krauts and make a circle with them so that they wouldn't be fired on."

Baum's men were almost there now. One by one they silenced the german machine guns. A Sherman thrust its way into the wire but for some reason couldn't break through. Its engine stopped and it hung there helplessly, like a gigantic metallic fly in some monstrous metallic spider's web. But there were others rumbling up the shell-pitted hill to take its place.

---

[5]As we shall see, there is a great deal of confusion about how many men died on the rescue mission. Official sources give a figure which is absurdly low; usually about nine dead. Yet Colonel Joe Matthews, one of the prisoners, remembers counting at least twenty-five who lay on the road to the camp.

"Bleibt da stehen!" Tech 5 Zeno snapped, suddenly re-
membering his German, forgetting he had sworn never to
speak that language—the language of the Nazis—ever
again. The old men of von Goeckel's camp guard snapped
an inquiring look at him. But they did as they were ordered, standing there in a wavering semicircle on the hillside around the American wounded, limbs trembling un-
controllably, shoulders bent as if the red-hot slugs that
struck the earth all around them were heavy summer rain-
drops and not the harbingers of sudden death.

Andy Demchak shot a swift glance at Zeno but said
nothing. All the time he had been with Dave he had been
unaware that the Tech 5 spoke fluent German.

But Zeno looked neither at Demchak nor the Germans.
He was too busy with the ever growing number of casualties. Sweat standing out in beads on his forehead, hands
dyed red with gore up to the wrists, he cut, tore, ripped
at the olive-drab of the wounded men's uniforms and got
on with the grim, painful business of repairing the
outrage which had just been violently inflicted on the
innocent white bodies revealed. Cut, sew, apply dressing,
sip of water and sulpha tablets. Cut, sew, apply dressing
. . . It went on and on, as if it would never end.[6]

Thus while the battle raged back and forth above them
on the summit of the hill, the two heroic medics worked on,
oblivious to the hell all around them, performing that job
of mercy that would one day earn them both the Silver
Star.

Back in the camp the kriegies packed the windows,
completely forgetting von Goeckel's threat, roaring their
heads off like kids at a football game. Occasionally a slug
or fragment of red-hot shrapnel would come whizzing
through the shattered windows and they would all duck
automatically. But the next moment they'd be up again,

---

[6]After the war David Zeno always maintained that only "twenty-
two men came back out of the 150 of my company." This figure,
as the author has already pointed out, strongly contradicts the
one released in the official bulletin of the Third Army.

shouting enthusiastic encouragement to the men of the 4th Armored battling outside to liberate them.

From the second floor of the camp's hospital Major Al Berndt, formerly of the 28th Infantry Division, and now the camp's surgeon, watched the progress of the attack with interest. But when heavy machine-gun slugs started to tear up the roof above him, his interest turned to alarm. Suddenly it struck him that the hospital was unmarked. Perhaps the Sherman might attack it, mistaking the important-looking structure for the German administration building.

Hurriedly he clattered down the stairs and ran to Goode's office. Breathlessly, he told Goode his problem and suggested that a team of doctors and corpsmen be set up in a second aid station at the other end of the building; a solid wall divided the place and there was no way of getting from one end to the other without running the risk of going outside.

Goode considered the suggestion and told him to get on with it. However, when Berndt left Pop's office, he had second thoughts, deciding it would be better to wait until the heavy artillery barrage had stopped. Thirty minutes passed. Still the camp had not been liberated. Neither had the aid station been set up. When Goode heard this, he was overcome by one of his sudden rages. He ordered Berndt sent for and asked for an explanation.

A nervous Berndt, more afraid of Goode than of the Germans, told him he didn't want to send his men out under fire. Goode flushed a deep red. To him Berndt appeared to have disobeyed an order, although the suggestion had come from the doctor in the first place. The medic's hesitation was damn rank insubordination, he told himself angrily. Glaring at the man, he said; "I am hereby relieving you of your duties as camp surgeon!"

Even in the midst of battle Pop Goode was running true to form.

A second Sherman now hit the wire. The posts held for one long moment. Then they buckled. The Sherman ground on in low gear, ripping the wire apart and pulling shreds along with it. Behind it the infantry started to scramble through the double fence in the tank's wake. Suddenly the lights went out in the camp. Some German had cut the cable in a last act of frustrated resistance. But the infantry weren't to be stopped now.

"The lights went out just before we got there," Sergeant Graham remembers. "We stormed through the double row of barbed wire with the tanks. Dismounted men went through the buildings releasing prisoners."

The kriegies, released at last, went wild with joy. The camp was abruptly transformed into a pandemonium of joyful, almost hysterical welcome. The freed officers jumped aboard the Shermans, shouting at the tops of their voices, pounding the men of the 4th on the back and hugging them in their exuberance.

"All the guys," Graham says, "began climbing on the tanks and kissing and hugging us. We had to push them off. They were in mixed uniforms. Some wore the clothes they had been captured in—even had blouses and pinks."

At that precise moment Father Cavanaugh was distributing Holy Communion, with his hands trembling so much that he feared he might drop the precious Host. As he came to the end of the line of men kneeling at the edge of the table, a series of loud cheers sounded from outside.

He turned to the altar and quickly finished the mass. Then he turned and asked, "What happened?"

"Father, we're free," several voices answered him gleefully.

"We're liberated! General von Goekel has surrendered."[7]

"Wasn't it wonderful," Major Fred Oseth, one of the congregation exclaimed, "While mass was going on, we were liberated! You're not a kriegie any longer, Father!"

But in the midst of the general jubilation, Captain Baum remained grim and unsmiling, letting his men joke and laugh and answer the kriegies' myriad questions. For his

---

[7] Von Goeckel hadn't surrendered. He was still in his command post to the rear of the camp.

part he kept back, concerned with the problem at hand: what was he going to do now?[8]

First, there were far more prisoners than he had anticipated and would be able to carry back even if all his tracked vehicles were available to transport them. And they weren't; he had already lost a goodly number.

Secondly, a quick glance around at the excited yet pale starved faces and skinny bodies of the men cluttering up his tanks told him that many of them wouldn't be able to walk—whatever they might think to the contrary—all the way back.

Thirdly—and this was the biggest headache of all— what was the way back?

This was the sixty-four-thousand-dollar question of the whole darned, confused situation.

Tired, worn, in pain from his wounds, a confused Captain Abe Baum got down to considering that particular problem after sending one of his typically laconic radio messages.

Received at divisional headquarters at 0300 hours on the morning of March 28, 1945, it said simply:

MISSION ACCOMPLISHED

It was the last message anyone was to receive from Task Force Baum. After that, there was nothing but silence.

---

[8] Most of the liberated kriegies I have talked to don't recollect Baum at all; at least they never met him at the time of the liberation of the camp.

Chapter 13

There comes a time in a battle when even the most experienced soldier makes a mistake. Sometimes it is made through illness. One thinks of Napoleon at Waterloo, plagued by dysentery, or Rommel at El Alamein, stricken by one of his violent headaches. Sometimes it is caused through nerves and worry as was the case with Ludendorf in August 1918. But in general the experienced soldier makes his big mistake through exhaustion, so that he is no longer capable of weighing the pros and cons and making a swift binding decision on the further conduct of operations.

And it was probably exhaustion that made Captain Baum sit on his tail for the next few precious hours while all about him in the darkened countryside the Germans prepared to deal him a death blow. Captain Abraham Baum simply wasted too much time at Hammelburg before he decided to move out.

Naturally he was human enough to want to rest on his laurels for a while. He had taken the camp after fighting and traveling (catching what little rest he could in the bucking jeep) for nearly thirty-odd hours. In the course of the fight through the enemy lines to Hammelburg he had lost half his force and now, after arriving at his objective, he found that he was burdened with far too many prisoners for his few remaining half-tracks to transport back safely to Allied lines sixty miles to the rear. His operation had been a tremendous success in that he had overcome all odds and taken Hammelburg. But at the same time it was a failure because he would not be able to get most of the "kriegies"—as he had already learned to call them—out of the POW camp. (He of course did not know that the real failure of the raid was that the man he had

140

come unwittingly to rescue lay seriously ill in the camp's hospital, incapable of being moved.)

Thus, exhausted and wounded, burdened with the terrible knowledge that he must soon tell the bulk of the noisy, excited POW's that he would have to leave them behind to become prisoners once more after he had left, the young American captain from the Bronx hesitated too long about his next course of action. Two hours too long, in the event.

While he waited about two miles from the camp, his task force in hopeless disorder from the overjoyed POW's who had ridden with them (who incidentally had completely given away his position by the huge celebration fires they had insisted on lighting), the German military machine started to swing into action. Their faces bright red and gleaming with sweat—in spite of the night air, which was beginning to grow cool—and their leg muscles threatening to burst from the strain of the forced march across the Franconian hills, the three hundred fanatical SS cadets had almost arrived at their objective. Now they were only a matter of miles away from Baum's force, somewhere in the darkness to the southwest.

To their left, Major Diefenbek had collected his scratch forces of combat engineers and whomever else he could round up and was now advancing on the unsuspecting Americans from the south. In the camp, Colonel Hoppe was also preparing to move out against the Americans as soon as armor arrived in the form of Koehl's remaining TD's. They were at Fuchsstadt, a few kilometers to Hoppe's south. Koehl had fed and rested his men and felt that by now they were capable of action again, their morale heightened by the knowledge that they had fought and beaten the Amis that afternoon. Although most of them hadn't been trained for night action, Koehl felt he could manage them well enough when and if the occasion should arise. One hour after Baum's men had broken into Hammelburg, German resistance had hardened; the enemy was now prepared to go over to the attack.

But in the camp the inmates knew nothing of this; they were still elated at their new-found freedom. After the kriegies had eaten the best meal most of them had had since being taken prisoner (a glorious mixture of potatoes, spam and fish, running with thick juicy grease), Goode ordered them outside ready for departure. Leaving behind them about one hundred kriegies, who were too ill to move, the laughing, jostling column, blankets wrapped across their bodies, precious souvenirs packed in make-shift packs,[1] stepped out at a sharp pace, their step electri-fied by the thought that every foot forward brought them closer to home.

As they marched down the Hermann Goering Strasse, for what they thought was the last time, the swarthy, hooked-nosed Serbs, who had looted the German armory and were now armed,[2] cheered them heartily. The kriegies cheered them back. The Serbs had been good to them, giving freely of their own precious stores of food when the Americans had none. They would always remember the Serbs.[3] A jubilant Father Cavanaugh cheered with them, waving his free hand in greeting; in the other he carried a flour sack, which a kind Serb had given him as a towel, filled with food and spare clothing.

Illuminated by the dying flames of the still burning Serbian hut, carefully stepping over the American dead, who lay crumpled around the wire in the careless attitudes of the violently killed, the column passed through the gap in the wire. With a proud and grateful Pop Goode at their head, the men started to march over the dark rough ground of the German artillery range toward the black silhouettes

---

[1] Even in the POW camp, the Americans were insatiable for souvenirs. General von Goeckel remembers one American doctor asking him for a "souvenir" and in order to humor the man, giving him a small silver drinking glass for "the kids." Twenty years later the astonished German received a picture showing the long-forgotten doctor surrounded by grown-up men, who were once the "kids," toasting him out of that very glass!

[2] The Serbs had armed themselves to prevent the Communist minority taking over the camp.

[3] Two of the Serbs, who had relatives in the States, went with the Americans.

of the 4th's tanks in the distance. Behind them the wooden gate of Oflag VII, which the liberated kriegies had torn half off its metal hinges in the first heady moments of their new found freedom, banged softly back and forth in the gentle wind which had suddenly sprung up . . .

The first German troops came in cautiously, slipping in and out of the deserted buildings in little silent groups like gray timber wolves in some remote forest. A platoon leader would dash forward at a crouch, hesitate a moment, breath held tensely while he peered to left and right in the gloom. Then he would wave carefully. Other gray shapes would appear. A similar pause and then they would push on. Weapons at the ready, they penetrated the Serbian compound.

A young Serbian lieutenant, armed with a looted French rifle, saw them first. For a moment he hesitated, then half raised his rifle. A look at the hard face of the leading German soldier, illuminated suddenly by a fresh spurt of flame from the burning buildings, changed his mind. He lowered the weapon. *"Lass das Ding fallen!"* the German ordered softly, the flames making his face appear bathed in sweat.

Again the Serb hesitated, not understanding the German.

The soldier raised his machine pistol, and the Serb understood. He dropped the rifle. The German half smiled and turning, waved his hand. More Germans appeared.

Frightened though he was, the Serb noted that these were not the old guards; these were young vigorous men from the German training camp up the road. They passed on.

Now Hoppe's men were everywhere. Von Goeckel left his command post, cornered the Serb general in charge of their compound and told him he wanted all looted weapons returned within the hour. *Otherwise*——He felt no need to complete the sentence; the threat posed by Hoppe's tough-looking snipers, their well-trained forefingers curled warily around the triggers of their rifles, was sufficient, he thought. The Serb seemed to agree. Within a matter of minutes his men had surrendered their looted weapons, piling them up in a heap on the parade ground of the compound. Simultaneously there was the noisy clatter of tank tracks in the distance. Moments later the great camouflaged hulk of the first Ferdinand TD, its metal deck crowded with infantry, hove into sight. Captain Koehl's tank destroyers had arrived.

Up on the high plateau where Baum's tanks lay in a loose defensive semicircle, the kriegies had grown silent. A little while before, two rifle shots had rung out in the darkness; Baum had ordered the fires put out at once. "No smoking and no lights!" he had yelled angrily, irritated by the prisoners' lack of discipline and happy unawareness of the sticky situation they were all in. Now the kriegies shivered in the cold and confined themselves to whispered conversations with their neighbors, while up the road near the command peep the young captain of the 4th and the old colonel Pop Goode conferred.

From the latter Baum learned for the first time the exact number of POW's in the American compound. The situation was worse than he had anticipated. Glumly he stared at the colonel's tough yet happy face. He had no alternative but to tell him. Feeling miserable, Baum broke the bad news.

Goode could have exploded when he heard that Baum had sufficient room for only a handful of the fittest prisoners who would be capable of riding on the decks of the Shermans and handling a weapon if necessary.

Why the hell had the fools back at Third Army launched the whole darn operation if they hadn't enough vehicles to get the rescued men out? he asked himself angrily. The man standing next to both of them could have answered that unspoken question if he had wanted to. But Major Alexander Stiller remained silent, preoccupied with his own thoughts. He had just learned that Waters had been badly wounded during the attack.

Goode looked at the exhausted face of the tall young infantry officer facing him and kept his temper. The youngster wasn't at fault; he had just carried out orders from the top.

"All right, Captain," Goode said. "I'll tell 'em the bad news."

The colonel soon rounded the kriegies together and then, with their faces looking up at him as he stood on the deck of a tank, gave them the news in his simple direct manner, hiding as best he could his rage at the whole damn fool business. He did not give them time to brood on the heartbreaking announcement he had just made, but got down straightaway to practical matters. Quickly he divided them into three groups: those who could escape on their own; those who felt they were fit enough to ride and fight with the tanks; and those who, like himself, would return to the camp, and wait for the day of their final liberation. "We have been liberated and are free. But until we can get within the American lines, each man is on his own. Sixty miles is the distance we will have to make—without food or supplies and we are in a weakened condition." He paused to let his words sink in and then concluded with the statement, "Each man is free to do as he thinks best."

Most of the men decided reluctantly to follow Pop Goode's example and with the colonel at its head, followed by a man bearing a large white flag, the sad procession started its slow way back across the rough fields to the still burning camp.

Others could not make up their minds. One such officer was Bruce Matthews, chaplain of the Disciples of Christ, who went up to his former commanding officer Colonel Seely and asked if he had any advice or orders.

"None, Chaplain," Seely replied, as if in a daze. "Each man is on his own."

"Do you have any advice to share?" Matthews persisted.

"None, Chaplain."

"Do you mind telling me what you plan to do, sir?" the chaplain asked earnestly.

"I'm going back in, Chaplain."

"Thank you, sir," the chaplain said and climbed on to the left fender of the nearest half-track.

Captain Alan Jones Jr., son of the commander of the

ill-fated 106th Division in the Battle of the Bulge, was not so lucky. With his feet still suffering from the effects of having them frozen during the long boxcar ride after his capture in the Schnee Eifel three months before, he was glad to have found a warm place on the engine of a Sherman. But his happiness was of short duration. The tank commander suddenly ordered off most of his passengers because they prevented his traversing his gun properly.

Many of the men who had still not got a place on the tanks ran up and down, pleading and begging—and even battling—for a place. The tankers sought desperately for extra room. All spare gear was dumped. Even their bed rolls were tossed overboard to make more space. But there was a limit to the room available, and those for whom there was no more space either followed the column back to the camp or sneaked off into the darkness to try their individual luck. In spite of the pain in his frozen feet, Jones was one of these, hobbling away slowly until he could be seen no more.

Sixty-five of the fittest of the kriegies were left and these were given spare weapons and told to make themselves useful. Baum was not sorry the rest had gone. They had cluttered up his column and temporarily destroyed his discipline. So much so that several German bazookamen had been able to infiltrate to within fifty yards and loose a few wild rounds at his tanks before making a hasty retreat. Now was the time to get his force back on the road. The men's wild enthusiasm had long since vanished. Both kriegies and the men of the 4th realized the dangers that lay between them and the return to their own lines. Like their commander, they were sober and grim, fully aware of the mess they were now in, their only real hope that there might be more 4th Armored men coming up from the Main to meet them.

Baum gave the order to "roll 'em." Readily the drivers switched on their engines and gunned them into life. Now all was hectic movement. Everyone was eager to get away. The first light recon tank moved off to find the road for the rest to follow. Task Force Baum was starting back.

"I didn't head in the same direction I came," Baum

remembers, "but started for the north with the hope of meeting up with another column. When we moved out I was told they were going in a northeasterly direction and I was to head that way."

Captain Baum did not know that he was heading straight into danger.

It was midnight.

At exactly midnight, Goode's men arrived back at the compound. Goode was fuming with rage. The Germans took him immediately to von Goeckel where he poured out his anger and disappointment. "I want no further part of this foolishness," he exploded to the general. "Those people [Baum's group] don't know what they're doing. They've lost all contact with the rear . . . I and most of my men prefer to stay here in the camp." Goode hesitated. "Will you take us back, General?"

If the occasion had not been such a serious one, the big German would have laughed. The question reminded him of all those old jokes of the ex-prisoner who, not being able to cope with the outside world, asks his former warden to take him back. But Goode's condition was too pathetic to be made fun of. Silently von Goeckel nodded his head.

The battered gate was swung back and the waiting column started in, watched by the disarmed Serbs, now sunk in voiceless dejection. Soon the gate clanged closed behind them and they dispersed. They were kriegies again.

Sadly Father Cavanaugh walked to his old barracks. "We're not free yet, Father," someone said wearily at his side.

"Well, let's get some sleep anyway," the chaplain said and entering, rolled onto his bunk.

Not for long, however. A few moments later someone shouted through the door, "The Germans are marching us out of here. Be ready in fifteen minutes."

As the first hour of the new day came to an end, five hundred kriegies were lined up on the Hermann Goering Strasse by forty German guards. Filling their pockets with moldy green potatoes—the only food they could find—

they allowed themselves to be herded through the gate once more and for the last time—never to return—they left Oflag VII and started down the steep road to the town of Hammelburg itself.

Staggering down the steep winding road, physically and spiritually exhausted by the events of the day, they could make out silent little groups of German infantry, waiting in the ditches on both sides, like gray ghosts.

Then came the roar of laboring automobile engines taking the steep gradient in low gear. Hurriedly their guards bullied the prisoners to one side to make way for the oncoming trucks carrying yet more infantry.

With sinking hearts the kriegies stared at the grim-faced, tense, helmeted Germans, pale blobs of faces visible in the blue convoy lights. They knew what these men were going to be used for: an all-out attack on Baum's pathetic, worn little force! As they moved back onto the road they could hear the rumble of tank tracks and the first dry faint crack of a German Panzerfaust.

Chapter 14

"We started back," Baum relates, "and hadn't gone fifty yards when we lost another tank to a bazooka. I had to change my direction so I took another compass reading and went to the southwest."

That decision slowed the force down. The route Baum had chosen was a tight-rutted farm track that grew steadily more and more difficult for his armored vehicles to cross. As the precious minutes ticked by, his progress became slower and slower.

Meanwhile, unknown to Baum, the German ring around his tiny force was becoming increasingly tighter. Somewhere in the darkness the three columns closing in on him were getting nearer and nearer and on every road within striking distance of the American task force tense German infantry waited behind hastily thrown-up barricades for the enemy to try to break through.

Within half an hour of their taking the rutted farm trail, it finally petered out altogether. Baum hesitated, while all around him in the darkness, enlivened only by the soft rythmic throb of his tank engines, his men waited tensely for his decision. "West," he ordered finally and obediently the column followed another trail in that direction. Soon faint tracks in the damp earth showed that other tanks had gone the same way and Baum, examining them, hoped that they were those of his recon group, which he had sent ahead.

They were, and shortly afterward a light tank appeared, bringing the good news that the recon boys had found a little road that ran to Hessdorf on the Würzburg-Hammelburg highway.

"Everything was fine until I crossed a bridge over the

149

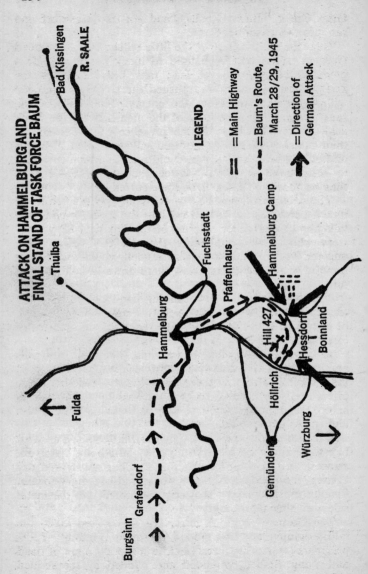

ATTACK ON HAMMELBURG AND
FINAL STAND OF TASK FORCE BAUM

LEGEND

══ = Main Highway

▪▪▪ = Baum's Route,
March 28/29, 1945

➤ = Direction of
German Attack

Giess Creek," Baum recalls, "and got into Hessdorf and ran into two road blocks."

Near the main square of the little village two abandoned German trucks had been used to block the road. For a moment the men on the lead tank hesitated, then the kriegies jumped down and pushed the trucks to one side without interference from the enemy. The noise of the tank's engines and the cries of the men heaving the truck aside woke the village to the presence of the enemy in their midst. "Amis!" the startled villagers cried in alarm and everywhere the frightened old men and women began to hang anything white—towels, sheets, shirts—out of their windows as a token of their surrender.

The column did not wait to enjoy any possible fruits of its easy conquest. It roared on into the night, leaving the villagers to the tender mercies of the fanatical SS youngsters who soon would pass through the village and, angered by the white flags of surrender, would round up a handful of the locals and mow them down in cold, savage fury.

The task force was now making good progress on the long straight road that led back to Hammelburg in spite of the frequent stops to allow the tanks and half-tracks to close up.

It was two o'clock in the morning. The lead tank was entering the little village of Höllrich and had just passed the shuttered *Gasthaus* before the church when the driver jammed on his brakes. In the darkness he had failed to spot the barricade thrown up across the road until it was almost too late.

The next instant the seemingly dead little village erupted into violent terrifying life. Stabs of violet-colored flame cut into the darkness. There was that familiar and feared dry crack of a bazooka and the shower of red-hot angry sparks. From both sides heavy projectiles slammed into the metal sides of the stalled tank.

The Germans couldn't miss. The first round killed the tank commander. The second scattered a group of ex-prisoners clear of its metal deck in a bloody mess of dead and dying. Stalled, wounded and blinded by the sudden

flame of the enemy bazooka, the panic-stricken driver of
the Sherman sprayed the little village street with 50-caliber
slugs, shooting crazily in every direction.

Enemy machine guns joined in. Small birds flew from
the trees on both sides of the road. Bullets crackled
through their branches like flames fanned by a great wind.
In the confused mess at the barricade, the Germans had
a perfect target. Everywhere men began to drop.

A German potato-masher grenade sailed heavily through
the blood-red night. It struck a tank, which was desperately
trying to turn about and get out of the trap. In a flash of
blinding ugly yellow light, it exploded, hurtling dead and
wounded kriegies from the deck, sweeping them away as
if by a waterhose, and leaving a few terrified men whimpering as they crouched closer to the protective armor.

Bursts of tracer and red flares which hushed high in the
night sky illuminated the desperate encounter. A large
house stood out, silhouetted among the trees, and a tracer
hitting the roof ricocheted and soared high. It seemed to
be the center of the German resistance, directing the machine-gun and small-arms fire which was rising to a crescendo.

Gradually the exhausted tankers began to react. Behind
the three fiercely burning Shermans, already knocked out,
they maneuvered for room to open fire, while someone on
one of the half-tracks started firing his 50-caliber. Angry
red and white tracer zipped flatly through the night in the
direction of the barricade. A white flare rocketed into the
night, pinpointing the German position in its icy white light.
Other machine guns joined in, viciously spraying both sides
of the streets with the messages of death. The kriegies
bailed out and, crouching in the gutter on either side of
the road, added their fire to the confused bloody mess at
the barricade.

And then abruptly it ended. The killing was over. The
German fire slackened off and, after firing a few last im-
potent rounds into the now silent darkness, so did the
American. Now all that could be heard was the rhythmic
throb of the Shermans' motors and the soft, hushed moans

of the wounded in the ditches and gutters, where the medics had dragged them.

Baum did some quick thinking, forcing his dog-tired brain to make a decision. Should he go on? In spite of the silence he knew the Kraut was still up the street waiting for him. No, that would be suicide. He no longer had the strength to force a decision against prepared positions. As he says himself, "I lost a tank commander and a large group of infantrymen . . . Knowing that I couldn't mess around there, I backed out of the area to assemble for reorganization on Hill 427, a mile east of Höllrich."

Thus an exhausted Baum took his sadly diminished little force back the way they had come till they began to crawl slowly up a trail they had discovered leading to the top of a hill feature numbered 427 on his map and which the locals called the "Reussenberg." It was the decision of a very tired soldier who sees an advantage in possessing "high ground" but who overlooks the fact that the very possession isolates him and leaves him wide open to encirclement. It was the same kind of fatal decision that another young dashing cavalry officer had made six decades before—General George Custer.

Up on the hill Baum took stock of his situation, rubbing his eyes constantly with a grubby, bloodied hand, trying to fight off the weariness. The kriegies, stimulated by the recent action, bombarded him with advice while he leaned weakly against a tank. Finally his nerve broke and he cussed them out angrily, telling them to "take off" if they wanted to. Indignantly a number did, going back down the hill to the highway. He never saw them again.

Stiller now ventured to get into the act. He (to use Patton's words after the action) "suggested that, instead of returning over the road already used, the column strike north. The officer in charge (Baum) declined that advice." Stiller retired, hurt, and Baum was left in peace to consider his situation.

It was lousy. He had started off with over 300 men, now —as he puts it—"I could barely scrape together two platoons, about 110 men. I had three mediums and three light tanks left, plus one command tank. The half-tracks were full of nonserious casualties and the infantry were on the tanks." This force, plus the sixty former prisoners who remained and his last 105, was the sum total of his offensive strength.

He now had but a few hours of darkness left in which to make his escape. But which way? His tired brain could see only one way—again through Höllrich. His decision made for better or worse, he got down to business.

I immediately got my people together and found out how much gas we had. I had enough gas for a 38- to 40-mile trip. We siphoned gas out of eight of the half-tracks to give us a greater driving radius. We destroyed the eight half-tracks by burning them.

When this task had been done, he assembled his battered little group on the top of the hill. By the light of the burning half-tracks their faces looked hollowed out, their eyes sunk deep into their skulls, their skin a sweaty red. Baum looked at them. There was none of the old drive and enthusiasm left in those faces. In these last forty-eight hours his men had seen too much action and too much death. Later he was to say of them:

Considering the condition of the troops when we left that night [the first night of the raid], I got results I never expected. There was never an order questioned throughout the whole trip and not a peep or squawk out of any of them. My enlisted men and officers were tops.

But now they were beat, and in spite of his wounds and his own exhaustion he knew he somehow had to give them their old sense of purpose. *He had to!* The words he used that night have not been recorded. But using all his powers of persuasion, he gave them what he calls laconically "a pep talk," urging them, cajoling them, threatening them into continuing their resistance. Then, after bedding down the seriously wounded in an old ruin they had found on the top of the hill and draping the area with a red cross fashioned from the brightly colored silk panels used for identifying Allied troops to their own pilots, Baum shouted the order to "mount up."

For one last time the tank motors roared into life, flooding the area with their blue fumes, while behind them against the dark, spiked silhouette of Hill 427 the sky began to flood a dirty white with the first tired light of the new day, and the first light tank commenced its cautious, hesitant progress down the hill. It was then that the Germans attacked in strength.

Chapter 15

0600 HRS
March 28

The German attack came in from three sides. From the direction of the camp, Koehl's great lumbering Ferdinands, supported by Hoppe's company of snipers, advanced cautiously to Baum's rear across the flat open country. From the south Diefenbek's engineers and the three hundred SS officer-cadets, spread out in a long line, advanced directly on the American positions, while from the northwest and northeast, what looked to Baum like the feared Tiger tanks were appearing over a low rise; great sinister low hulks, which could only mean death. Baum was completely trapped. There was no earthly means of escape. The tragedy of his last stand could begin.

Covered by artillery fire, the Germans attacked at once. Abruptly there was that sound like silk being ripped, followed seconds later by a loud flat crack which indicated that the Germans were using their most feared weapon—the long-barreled 88 cannon. Moments later came the furious burr of the 20-mm anti-aircraft guns being used in an infantry support role. The rate of fire was stupefying.

As Baum remembers it: "They hit us with the fastest tank fire I had ever seen. It was like automatic fire." Within a matter of minutes the morning stillness had vanished. In its place was the terrifying, ungodly howl of shell and shrapnel.

To the frightened men huddled with heads down by the vehicles it seemed that it would never end. The double boom of the explosions. The flat silk-ripping of the shell. The high brown fountain of earth and dirt, that pattered down like heavy rain on their helmets. The hot angry rush of shrapnel zigzagging among the dying trees, amputating their branches and leaving behind fresh white scars

in the wood. The burning half-tracks made the little task
force a perfect target and the German gunners were having a field day. Tank after tank was hit, exploding with the
hellish crump and hot searing flame that come when a
gasoline engine is struck.

Desperately Tech 4 Alfonso Casanova, a small swarthy
Texan, fought his 105 to the last. Working feverishly
against time, the commander ordered his gun crew to lay
smoke to hide the trapped task force. Too late. A German
88 slugged into the side of the vehicle. Casanova, his gunner Jack Stanley and the assistant gunner Lawrence White
fell back wounded. Frantically they struggled to their feet
from the chaotic debris at the bottom of the vehicle. They
continued to fire smoke. Another direct hit struck them,
rocking the gun from side to side and wounding the two
gunners once again. They were out for good. Casanova
fought on alone. Loading the gun himself, he fired round
after round, standing in the slippery blood and gory confusion of the 105. Then Casanova got his. A German 88
struck the vehicle its death blow. At last the big assault
gun was silent.

Then, as suddenly as it had started, the heavy barrage
stopped, leaving Baum's armored vehicles a smoking, burning mass of metal. The infantry were coming in to finish
the job.

With professional interest, Baum noted that "up to this
time I had never seen the Krauts pull a good coordinated
attack with artillery cover and tanks backing up the infantry the way they should." Now he was seeing it for the
first and the *last* time in his fighting career.

Behind the lumbering tanks, their guns swinging from
side to side, vicious multicolored flames spouting from
their cannon at regular intervals, the SS men crouched,
bayonets fixed. They came on at a steady determined pace,
slowing up a little as they hit the foot of the hill. Over their
heads came the pop-pop-pop of the heavy machine guns
which filled the air with the bright morse code of tracer
and which was intended to keep the Americans flat with
their faces in the dirt. It succeeded with most of them. But
not all.

Major Don Boyer, captured three months before at St.-Vith, was now in action again. Crouched over the 50-caliber machine gun of one of the Shermans, he was enjoying himself for the first time since his capture. He sped an angry hail of lead at the advancing infantry. But not for long. A shell struck the Sherman, turning it into a blazing torch. Hurriedly he abandoned his gun and fled into the woods.

The SS men were getting nearer.

His face gray-glazed with fatigue in the light of the furiously burning tanks, Baum ordered his men to withdraw into the woods higher up the hill. They needed no urging. Ignoring the lead which was tearing through the trees, everywhere, they fled into the cover afforded by the wood higher up. It was a mad scramble with every man for himself.

The SS infantry were close now. They were spraying the area Baum had just vacated with machine pistols, dodging from tank to tank, firing from the hip as they ran.

Desperately, Baum tried to regain control of the situation. With a group just as desperate as himself, he ran down the hill to where the Shermans were burning fiercely, the flames crackling hungrily upward into the morning air, and tried to break through. No good. Every time they broke out of the trees, the SS men hit them with all they had. "We tried to get back to see what we could salvage out of the mess," Baum remembers, "but each time we showed our faces, the infantry opened up with small arms and the advancing tanks started firing again." Frantically they fled back to cover, leaving their dead and dying behind them, fighting each other to get out of the way of that murderous fire.

Task Force Baum was about finished.

In the end Baum decided it was no good trying to fight back as an organized body. His group was finished as a disciplined unit. Now it was a case of the old motto: *sauve-qui-peut*. Raising his voice above the chatter of the machine guns, he yelled to the frightened, exhausted men crouching all around him in the wood, "Break up in groups of four and take off!"

Every man for himself. In frantic haste what was left of the force broke up, each man seeking a buddy he felt he could trust most. Giving his men a few more hasty directions, Baum motioned to Stiller to follow him and, with another kriegie, they broke into the thickest part of the pines and started to run for it. In the far distance they could hear the Germans detonating TNT as they blew up more bridges so that the Baum force couldn't escape that way. Closer at hand, they heard another sound which made their blood run cold. Faintly but definitely, they could hear the low baying of animals. The Germans were bringing up the hounds from the camp. Their lungs threatening to burst with the exertion, the three men blundered on crazily through the underbrush.

As the first light of day revealed a hillside littered with wrecked, smoldering half-tracks and tanks among the battered debris of the shell-shattered wood which marked the graveyard of Task Force Baum, half a hundred frightened, hounded Americans fled the Germans' wrath. Some were helmetless, some weaponless, but they were all determined, wounded or not, to escape and, in the case of the kriegies, never again to suffer the misery and hunger of a German POW camp. But the enemy was equally determined to find the last survivors of this impudent raid so deep behind their lines.

By midmorning the hunt was in full swing. Down on the road that ran south from Hammelburg, the Germans had placed tanks at intervals with patrols of infantry to link them up, so that if the Americans ventured out of the thickly wooded Reussenberg area and tried to cross the road, (which they must do if they wanted to take the quickest way back to their own lines) they would be picked up. Up on the hill the SS men, triumphant at the defeat they had inflicted on the Amis, worked deeper and deeper into the forest, led on by the excited, baying hounds.

All day long they continued to have success, plodding through the heavy underbrush or fighting through the thick pines to winkle out yet another sullen, ragged prisoner, who would be forced down the hill at the end of some grinning private's bayonet.

Like hunted animals the Americans doubled and redoubled their tracks trying to avoid their pursuers, lying buried in the undergrowth, their heads deep in the dirt, hardly daring to breathe, vainly hoping that that bellow of triumph and that harsh command, *"Komm raus, Mensch!"* would never come. It always did.

Dave Zeno was almost at the end of his tether. The last thirty-six hours had about finished him. Together with a young Italian private, whose name he never learned, his uniform bloodied with the gore of a dozen dead and dying, he blundered through the undergrowth, with the sound of the baying hounds lending haste to his tired feet.

"Where now?" the young Italian panted, his dark Latin eyes eloquent with fear as they sought some reassurance in the older man's face. Zeno tried to control his heaving chest. His breath was coming in short, harsh gasps. His lungs threatened to burst. "There's a road—somewhere—somewhere down there! Come on—quick!"

Together they stumbled on, the branches lashing at their gaunt, stricken faces. On and on. The sound of the dogs was getting ever louder. Desperately Zeno forced himself on. The road to Würzburg couldn't be much farther away. Once across that, they might have a chance of breaking through the German cordon and getting to their own troops advancing from the west. He must not be captured. He was a Jew. He'd never go to a POW camp. They'd shoot him out of hand.

Then suddenly he saw the wood was beginning to peter out. Down below, Zeno could just see the bare shining snake of the main road. "Look," he grasped his companion's arm, "that's the road . . ."

He got no further.

The Italian was staring as if hypnotized over his shoulder.

Slowly, very slowly, Zeno turned.

Two German soldiers were rising triumphantly from the

bushes a dozen yards away, their rifles pointing directly at the two Yanks.

Then David Zeno's heart almost stopped beating. He recognized one of them. *It was a kid he had gone to school with!* Slowly and fearfully he began to raise his hands.[1]

Sergeant Donald Graham, the lone survivor of the brave last stand put up by the 105's, had taken off with three other enlisted men. Two miles away from the site of the disaster they had bumped into a German patrol. The three other men ran *up* the hill. It was a split-second decision of exhausted men, too tired now to think straight. It was a fatal one. The Germans spotted them at once. The leading Kraut let loose a burst. Up on the hill the three men were too good a target. The lead hissed through the bushes all around them, kicking up little spurts of dirt. Quickly they came to a halt. Reluctantly they raised their hands.

"Old head" Graham did the opposite. "I went up a draw and was concealed by woods," he remembers about that hectic day. He got away. By nightfall he was clear of the immediate German pursuit, alone in the thickly wooded hilly Franconian countryside. Every man's hand was against him now, he knew, and he was feeling the first pangs of the hunger that was going to plague him over the next five lonely days, but at least he was free.

Major Stiller, Captain Baum, a young tank lieutenant and a couple of enlisted men weren't so lucky. They evaded capture most of the day, but by evening the pursuit was closing in on them. Panting heavily, their breath coming in harsh stacatto bursts, they were just about to cross a dirt trail in the forest when Stiller grabbed hold of Baum's arm. "Look, there's a cart," he whispered urgently. Baum tensed and crouched to the ground. The others followed his example.

A small wooden cart drawn by two ancient nags was parked right there on the trail directly in front of them. On it sat two German soldiers.

---

[1] Fortunately for Zeno, the German didn't recognize him and the American survived the war.

"What are we going to do now?" Stiller asked anxiously.

At a loss, Baum racked his tired brain for some way out. Behind them the baying of the German dogs was getting louder.

They could only go forward!

Then suddenly the Germans made the decision for them. The bigger of the two—a sergeant—spotted them. Quickly he grunted something to his companion and then, jumping down from the cart, the rifle on his shoulder striking its side, he dragged a small pistol from the holster at his side and aimed it at the bushes which concealed the Americans. Then, with Baum not more than twenty-five feet away, he placed one hand on his hip as if he were on some peace-time range and, taking deliberate aim, fired.

The bullet hit Baum's abdomen, ripping away his fly. Baum fell back, blood streaming from his belly and leg. "Goddammit," he exploded angrily, the sharp pain welling up inside him, "you son-of-a-bitch, you've shot my nuts off!"

The German sergeant, who obviously understood English, laughed uproariously,[2] and with a gesture of his thirty-eight directed that Baum should throw away his grease gun and come out. Quickly Baum tore off his badges of rank and his dog tags which indicated that he was Jewish and threw them deep into the bushes. Then he dropped his grease gun and with Stiller's aid raised his one good hand and came out.

The Germans frisked them[3] and then herded them into a barn with six other captives. There Able did a bit of quick reckoning. There was one guard for the lot of them. And he still had his helmet. He looked at Stiller and the

[2] Later the sergeant told Baum that he had been born in Bridge-port, Conn. In other words, he was a native-born American who had volunteered for the German Army because he sympathized with the Nazi creed.

[3] Under his mackinaw Baum had another pistol hidden which he kept for the next eight days while imprisoned in Hammelburg. After his wounds had been treated by the Serbian doctors and he felt in better shape, he was just about to escape when the camp was liberated.

other guys. They still looked as if they could run a bit further. The old spirit was still there.

Swallowing hard and summoning up the last of his strength, he slipped off his helmet and took a firm grip on its edge. Clenching his jaw in determination, he was just about to hit the unsuspecting German guard over the head with it, when Stiller grabbed his wrist. All the fight fled from Baum's body. At last the young captain, who had fought his men so far these last two days, gave in.

"I could hardly walk and was partly carried. I was convinced I had enough for a while."

Supported by Stiller and another man, he was trailed down the road to Hundsfeld. There the confusion was so great that nobody bothered to search the prisoners and, although the Germans tried to separate the 4th Armored from the kriegies, a few of these convinced the enemy that Baum was an escapee. In his place a protesting Major Stiller was led away as the leader of the task force.

Baum continues his story:

We were evacuated to the town of Hundsfeld—and from there we were marched back to the prison camp. Being wounded I managed to get into a building that night while the other prisoners were being taken away . . .

Some prisoners who had been in the camp and knew the ropes told the Krauts I was one of the group that had escaped from the camp and that I should be sent to a hospital as I couldn't walk. Before I knew it, a Kraut woke me up and sent me by truck to a Serbian hospital at the POW camp. When I got to the hospital I found some 35 of the men who were wounded in my operation and recaptured.

In the darkness the thrice-wounded young captain from the Bronx was left alone with his thoughts. The raid had not succeeded. All the effort, the blood, the heroism, the dying had been in vain. Angrily he told himself that it had all ended in bloody failure. He had not been able to pull it off! All the confidence that Abrams and Cohen had placed in him, all the high hopes with which he had set out—seemingly—so long ago had been to no avail. He had failed. Lying there in drowsy pain, his anger was made more poignant by the soft moans of the wounded in the dark all around him.

We do not know whether Captain Baum asked himself why the raid had been ordered in the first place that March night. He was young and headstrong, and his temperament wasn't given to recrimination or meditation. Very probably he did not succumb to such thoughts. Finally the 24-year-old officer who had fought one of the strangest and most daring missions of the whole war drifted off into exhausted yet troubled sleep.

That evening just before dark, a lone American fighter, searching for Task Force Baum at Patton's express command, spotted a convoy of German trucks heading for the Hammelburg camp. Eager for information, the young fighter-pilot zoomed down low over the slow-moving ponderous trucks, finger close to the button that operated his eight machine guns. He did not know it, but the trucks had been ordered to the Oflag to take away the remaining kriegies and what was left of Baum's men. Wondering whether he should shoot them up or not, the pilot raced over the length of the convoy. Then hastily he removed his finger from the firing button.

A large white sheet was spread out in a field to the convoy's front. The pilot throttled back. Spelled out on the white sheet were five black letters:

USPWS

For a moment his brain refused to register the information. Then he tumbled to their meaning: United States Prisoners of War.

Down below, tiny black figures began to wave to him, white faces standing out against the blackness. They were the last survivors of Task Force Baum. The pilot immediately waggled his wings in recognition and banked to the west. In a matter of seconds he was a black spot on the horizon. A moment later he was gone altogether and the miserable men crouched below in the wet field were alone. The forty-eight hours were over.

Part Three

The End Of An Old Warrior

xxxxxxxxxxxxxxxxxxxxxxxxxxxxx

There is a species of whale which is said to spend much of its time lying on the bottom of the deepest part of the ocean. I don't mind saying at the present moment I feel lower than that whale's arse!

General George S. Patton Jr.,
to his staff (May 15, 1945)

Chapter 16

A battle does not end when the echo of the last shot has finally vanished into the surrounding hills or fields. Just as when a stone is thrown into a pond and the ripples spread outward and outward seemingly continuing for ever, so it is with a battle. For some it means a lifetime chained to a chair, thinking and rethinking that awful moment when it happened and the mangled mess that was once legs lay on the ground ten yards away. For some it is the tortured nightmares and wakening, bathed in sweat, the fevered cries and commands of years before still echoing in the dark passages of the mind. And for a few, it is a man's sudden decision that ends swiftly in the blinding, life-extinguishing flash of a revolver fired at his own head.

In the month that followed the big raid, the ripples spread far and wide. Captain Fuchs was killed almost immediately as he escorted prisoners farther into the interior. Colonel Hoppe, who had organized the final attack on Hill 427, gave way to despair and shot himself within days of his triumph. Captain Koehl's TD's, which had contributed so much to that success, rumbled to the front a day or so later and disappeared into the avalanche of the Third Army advance that was now roaring over central Germany.

But if the fate of the German participants in the last desperate action was grim, that of some of the Americans who took part was little better. Take that of Sergeant Donald Graham, for instance, starved and ragged, his eyes large and wild like those of a hunted animal, wandering through the alien wilderness of the Spessart Mountains.

Sergeant Graham had been running five days now, and he was desperate for something to eat. That night he spotted a farmhouse and, his hand clutching his pistol, decided to risk it. The gnawing pain in the pit of his stomach overruled every other consideration. Cautiously he made his way up some concrete steps. Then abruptly his heart almost stopped beating. Someone else was coming down!

He pressed himself against the nearest wall, hoping that the darkness would hide him. It did. A civilian—probably the farmer—and three soldiers passed him by so closely that he could have reached out and touched them. After that—as he recalls—"I wasn't hungry any more."

On the sixth day Graham knew he was close to the front. Amidst the heavy rumble of the artillery—the background music of the war which was always there—he could hear the lighter crack of small artillery pieces and chatter of machine guns. Exhilarated at the thought that he must be getting close to friendly troops, he pushed on through the woods with renewed energy. Some time later he blundered into the Germans. Tired and hungry as he was, the ragged NCO reacted more swiftly than the three surprised men facing him in the middle of the lonely wood.

"*Hände hoch!*" he snapped, grabbing his forty-five.

The Germans obeyed smartly.

Graham eyed the three men cautiously. They were all officers, two of them—as far as he could tell—high-ranking ones. With a motion of his pistol he told them to come forward—slowly.

They did so and one of them said hesitantly in fair English, "We surrender."

Graham, sure of himself now, told the officer there was nothing else for them to do.

"I asked him what troops were attacking in this vicinity," Graham recalls, "and he told me he didn't understand. I asked him for his pistol, maps and dispatch case. He handed them to me. I told him that if he understood this far, he could continue understanding."

To emphasize his words, the lone sergeant pulled the hammer back on his pistol and asked again what troops were attacking.

The German gave in.

"He told me that Americans were here with some Panzers and quite a bit of infantry. He said there were no German troops around, so I told the three officers to beat it."

The German was lying.

A little later Graham spotted a tank firing. Figuring that if he came out in front of it, "I'd get mowed down," he approached it from the rear.

On its side it had a large black cross and it was firing at an American TD in the distance! It was German all right.

As he watched, two men got out of the tank and started running up a nearby hill. They were followed by a score of German infantry. Graham suddenly panicked. He hadn't come so far and gotten so close to his own lines to be shot in some anonymous little skirmish. He fled up the hill after them.

"When I got to the top I got weak and couldn't move any further. A German motorcyclist came by and killed his motor right by me and I really got scared."

He passed on.

A few moments later Graham caught sight of a company of infantry working their way cautiously through the wood, as if they were searching it. At a crouch, Graham ran to their flank, scared they were Germans looking for him.

Suddenly one of the infantry spotted him and the pistol in his hand. "Come on out, you Kraut son-of-a-bitch!" the man called angrily.

They were GI's!

But Sergeant Donald Graham's troubles were not yet over.

"I'm American," he yelled, overjoyed to be through the enemy lines at last.

"Don't give us that crap!" the GI yelled back. "Throw down that goddam pistol!"

Graham hurried over to the suspicious infantry (they were from the 45th Infantry Division which had assaulted Aschaffenburg) and showed them his dog tags.

They weren't convinced. There was muttered talk of shooting the "spy son-of-a-bitch."

As Graham put it later, "That's when I got to feel uneasy. They asked me who was my division commander, army commander, battalion CO, platoon leader, and really gave me a workout."

While Graham sweated, frantic with worry that he was going to be put against the nearest tree and shot by his own people (he knew from experience that frontline troops were not overly nice in their treatment of suspects), they continued their interrogation—"about maneuvers, where I sailed from, where I landed in France and the different towns we had taken."

Finally they were convinced and sent him back to battalion headquarters, where a captain handed him a canteen cup of coffee and a cup of pineapple, his first food for six days, and told him not to eat too much.

Graham didn't, but even so, "When I ate that it gave me the cramps."

Sergeant Graham had had a tough time, but he had survived. Some of the members of that ill-fated raid were not so lucky.

On the same day that Sergeant Graham finally broke through to the Allied lines, a lone line of ragged prisoners from Hammelburg trudged through Nuremberg, ideological home of Nazism and soon, in 1946, to be the scene of its death as well. In spite of the tremendous pounding that the site of the prewar Nazi rallies had taken from Allied bombers over the last three years, the city still functioned.

Tired and worn as they were, the kriegies looked around them with interest. This was the first big German city most of them had seen since their capture months before.

Mostly the citizens walked, or rode decrepit bicycles through the piles of rubble which lined virtually every street, but here and there an ancient car chugged by, powered by a wood-burning motor in the trailer that it towed. The factories were functioning too. All the intensive bombing by Lancasters at night and Flying Fortresses by day hadn't stopped their production of weapons for Hitler's armies. Depressed by what they saw and the thin cold drizzle which had been falling on them all morning, the prisoners trudged on.

As the column reached the other side of the city, the rain stopped and the skies cleared. Up front the NCO's gave the order to halt and told the Americans they could fall out; they had an hour to eat. Gratefully the POW's sprawled on the grass and began to unpack their bits and pieces of food. Father Cavanaugh joined them, stretching out under some spruce trees and enjoying the warm rays of the welcome spring sun.

Shortly before noon, the resting men could hear the long wail of what the Germans called the *"Vorwarnung"* coming from the direction of the city. Allied planes had been spotted. The POW's looked up with curiosity, but without concern. The "forewarning" simply meant enemy planes were about, but it didn't mean that Nuremburg was going to be the object of their attack.

Suddenly the long thin wail changed to short alarming blasts. The kriegies' mood changed. "Hey, let's get going," someone said nervously. The German NCO's began to scan the sky anxiously. This was ideal weather for low-level bombing by the Ami *jabos* (fighter-bombers).

Half a mile away there was the long metallic glint of the railroad, reflecting the April sunshine, and beyond that long low rows of factories, intersected here and there by storage tanks. All in all, an ideal target for bombers.

Scores of Germans started to run from the factories, cross the lines and head for the POW's. Some of them shouted, but they were too far off to be understood. The kriegies looked at them in bewilderment and one of them yelled amused, "Gee, look at those Jerries run!"

Then Father Cavanaugh spotted the cause of the Germans' alarm. High up in the bright spring sky, two lines of dark objects were roaring down on them, growing larger and larger by the second.

Bombers!

Now they split up, coming in from south and west. Marker flares mushroomed out of the leading planes and began to sink slowly to the ground, directly above the reclining POW's. Suddenly the POW's tumbled into action. *"My God, we're on the target!"* a panic-stricken voice yelled.

The priest leaped to his feet. He knew he must prevent a general panic. "Make the Act of Contrition!" he shouted above the roar of the planes. Hastily he rapped out the words of the General Absolution, while the bombs began to whistle down over the factories. Then, falling to the ground, he pulled a blanket over his head and prayed.

The first bombing took a couple of minutes, but to Cavanaugh it seemed like years. But finally there was a lull and he raised his head to take a cautious look at the smoking factories.

"Keep yer head down!" someone bellowed.

The second flight of bombers was approaching.

They came and went, leaving a trail of death behind them. More followed. And yet more. The noise was deafening. Screams, bombs, explosions, flak—they all merged into one overwhelming din that threatened to go on forever.

This must be the end, the priest told himself as he peered out through the dust cloud all around at the men who hugged the shuddering earth which jumped up and down beneath them rhythmically. But it wasn't. The last flights were directly overhead. Their bombs came rushing down. Great brown streams of earth and gravel fled into the sky and came raining down on the cowering men a moment later. Huge gleaming shards of steel bomb-shrapnel came flying through the air. Men were being hit everywhere. The morning was full of their screams.

Deafened and completely bewildered by the disaster, the priest got to his feet and started anointing every still form he could find, running from one to another till he got to the head of the column. Then it struck him that he might have missed some. He started back, walking this time, the noise of the bombers' engines dying in the distance. "Back to their goddam ham and eggs!" someone cried in cynical despair.

"Father, come and help us get this man," a kriegie

shouted. Cavanaugh turned. An officer was staring down at a wounded comrade, lying in a water-filled crater. Five other officers were gaping down at the moaning man in blank, uncomprehending bewilderment.

"Come on, get busy," the priest yelled at them. "Help out, I have other work to do!"

He went up to one of his former "parishioners" at Hammelburg, Jimmy Losh. The officer was lying on his stomach, attended by his pal Jim Keogh.

"He got it in the side, Father," Keogh said softly.

Cavanaugh looked down at the bloodstained GI shirt wrapped around the man's body to keep his intestines in and knew he was dying. He gave him Absolution and tried to console the dying officer.

"Do you think I'll be all right, Father?" Losh asked weakly.

"I sure hope you will. We'll get a doctor here for you in a few minutes."

He moved on.

Another former "parishioner" of his lay on the edge of a bomb crater, with two other officers tying pieces of a bloodied shirt around what was left of his shattered leg.

"Well, Father, it looks as if I'm not going to make it," the wounded man said and managed a grin. He pointed to a severed leg, with the boot still on, a few yards away. "That's part of me over there."

Captain John Madden came up to the group. "One of the Protestant chaplains has been killed. They want you to come over."

Feeling himself getting weaker at every step, Cavanaugh followed the captain to where the chaplain lay crumbled in death. It was Chaplain Koskamp. As Cavanaugh stooped to anoint him, he saw that there was already an oily cross drawn by someone's thumb on the dead man's dirty forehead.

Slowly the group reorganized. The guards marched the survivors away from Nuremberg while the remaining chaplains and doctors took care of the rest. Working among the rubble and the carnage, the chaplains laid out the dead—over a score of them—in neat rows, while the three surviving doctors took care of the nearly hundred wounded. Then, exhausted and heavyhearted, they sank into the rubble to rest.

A German NCO, who had stayed behind to guard the little group, asked Cavanaugh for a cigarette. He gave him one, when suddenly the world seemed to swing giddily all about him. The priest felt himself falling. Then everything went red and then black. Oblivion.

The next thing Father Cavanaugh knew, somebody was raising his neck and feeding him sips of water out of a canteen. It was the German sergeant. Slowly, shaking his head to remove the last traces of the faint, the priest sat up. Wordlessly he and the German stared at the rows of dead men, their feet sticking up from the rubble. The ripples were spreading wider and wider.

On the morning after the bombing of the POW's in Nuremberg, General von Goeckel, still in Hammelburg, was a worried man. He had just received orders from Army headquarters in Nuremberg to retreat with his remaining men. Now he was to go, presumably to be forced into one of the many last-ditch companies being formed everywhere by the SS out of odds and sods like his own men. But what was going to happen to his wife when he left, alone save for the handful of other women, and surrounded by men who had not had a woman for years and had—to boot—every reason to hate the Germans?

At two o'clock that morning he sent for Major Berndt, the American doctor, who had been reinstated by Colonel Goode before he left and ordered to look after the wounded. Quickly the German general briefed the American on the situation. The Americans were approaching the camp rapidly; Goeckel would be taking off with the remaining guards that morning; Berndt would then be in charge of the kriegies still remaining in the camp—some seventy in all.

Berndt could scarcely conceal his joy. Finally they were going to be freed—and this time for good! But von Goeckel did not notice the look of happiness on the

American doctor's face. He was too preoccupied with his own problems.

Drawing in his breath with his customary difficulty, he said slowly, "I would like to ask a favor."

Berndt nodded, wondering what was coming.

Von Goeckel pointed to the building which housed the cell-like room he occupied with his wife. "In that house I am leaving my wife and sister-in-law. I ask you to accept personal responsibility for their safety, mainly because of the Russian camp which will be liberated soon after this camp."

Berndt agreed readily. That morning he would have agreed to anything.

Shortly afterward, the tall, broad figure of General von Goeckel left the camp for the last time at the head of his silent, dejected middle-aged guards.

Once he had gone, Berndt placed his two other doctors on guard over the general's home, and then sat down in the hospital among the wounded, including Baum and Waters, waiting impatiently for the relief force as the boom of the guns grew louder and louder.[1]

From the same spot where a week before he had watched Baum's force battle its way into the camp, Berndt watched the new attempt at relief. It was a thrilling sight for him as the tanks of the 14th Armored Division came charging across the fields, firing as they came. Two of his men broke out a large Red Cross and an American flag they had painted themselves for just this eventuality with the aid of mercurochrome and methylene blue. The tanks spotted the flags almost at once and the firing died away immediately. The first Sherman then hit the wire and pressed on, dragging the wire and poles behind it. The Serbs swarmed out of their huts, cheering wildly and throwing their little rimless caps in the air. Some wept for joy and Berndt remembers that one man even kissed the

---

[1] After the Americans had left, the Serbs volunteered to take over the guarding of Frau von Goeckel's house, but when they left, the house was plundered by new American troops. Frau von Goeckel wasn't to see her husband again until two years later.

dusty side of the Sherman in an ecstasy of emotion. Hammelburg was free at last! And this time for good.

Berndt didn't waste time. His wounded needed attention badly. The Serbian chief surgeon, Colonel Danovich had done an excellent job, but he simply had not had the equipment to take care of the more seriously wounded, including Waters, whom Berndt feared might be paralyzed. He straightaway got in touch with Colonel James Lann[2] of the 47th Tank Battalion who had led the rescue force, and told him of the situation. Waters, in particular, needed attention badly and Berndt added significantly, "He's Patton's son-in-law, you know." That did it.

The news was flashed to Third Army HQ. Immediately Charles Odom of Patton's staff was detailed to fly Waters out. Thus, while the rest of the wounded waited to be evacuated through "normal channels," the man for whom the whole operation had been executed was flown to the 34th Evacuation Hospital at Frankfurt.

On the morning of April 7, General Patton drove to see Waters in the hospital. Patton was both moved and shocked by the condition of his favorite son-in-law, whom he had not seen for two long years. He wrote to his daughter, 'Little B', immediately afterward: "Johnny is awfully thin, but his morale is good and he is going to pull through."

Colonel Waters' morale was good because the doctors had just told him he was not going to die or be paralyzed. Yet in spite of his happiness at this great news, he was troubled.

Since the raid, he had been in bed most of the time, but although the words had never been spoken in his presence, he sensed what Berndt and the others in the hospital had been thinking all along. Now he looked up at his father-in-law's tough yet at this moment gentle face, and asked weakly, "Did you know I was in Hammelburg?"

Patton hesitated and then spoke. "No, I did not!"

Waters noted at that moment how old his father-in-law

---

[2] Lann had been one of Baum's instructors at OCS.

had grown in these last two years. There was a lot of gray among the close-cropped hair now, deep dark circles ringed his eyes and there were wrinkles around the mouth which had not been there in Tunisia so long ago.

"I knew there were American POW's in the camp and that's why I went in."

Waters smiled his understanding and relaxed. He was glad he was not the cause of the whole sorry mess.

The tall Third Army Commander sat in straight-backed silence and stared down at Waters' thin, deathly pale face. We don't know what went through his mind at that moment (it is not recorded), but we do know that this was to be the first of General George S. Patton's many evasions about Task Force Baum and the raid on the Hammelburg camp. The ripple had finally reached the man who had thrown the stone into the water.[8]

---

[8] One day later after this interview Colonel Waters was evacuated to a hospital in Paris. On the 8th, Patton again visited his son-in-law in company with Mr. John McCloy, the Assistant Secretary for War, who had given Patton a great lift by telling him: "One advantage you have over other generals is that you *look* like a General!" After McCloy had gone, Patton returned to Waters and pinned the Silver Star and Oak Leaf Cluster on him. "He did not know that he had been awarded either decoration, having not lived, in an historical sense, for more than two years, since his capture in Tunisia" [Patton writes]. Soon thereafter Waters was flown to the States.

Chapter 17

It was the German news reports, intercepted by the various Allied monitoring units in France and the United Kingdom, and passed on to the press as a matter of routine, which first roused the interest of the correspondents attached to the Third Army. In the last days of March, the reports of an American armored unit shot up and possibly exterminated by the Germans far behind their lines began to filter through (Reuters first reported the event on March 29) and the journalists began to ask questions: What was the unit? What was it doing so far behind the enemy lines? What has happened to it?

Patton, at his new headquarters in the suburbs of the much-bombed German town of Frankfurt, became alarmed when the newspapermen, scenting they were onto a story, began to press for information about this strange expedition.

Hastily he empowered his press officer to make a statement. The Third Army spokesman gave out a vague release about a "4th Armored Divisional raiding expedition" sent out "southeast toward Nuremberg." There was no mention of Hammelburg and no convincing explanation as to the purpose of the "raiding expedition."

The correspondents weren't satisfied.

Back at Hoge's 4th Armored Divisional HQ deep in Saxony the lower-ranking staff officers in the know began to mutter when they finally realized that the two companies would never be coming back. Already on the 29th and 30th the handful of scared, wild-eyed survivors who had managed to stagger back to General Patch's Seventh Army lines had told their harrowing story of that last stand on Hill 427. The angry muttering spread to Eddy's corps HQ and, try as he might, Eddy could not prevent it "traveling the grapevine to Army Group," as General Bradley put it later, when he explained how he first learned of the "wild goose chase"—his own description of the Hammelburg raid.

The correspondents' interest grew. They began to ask more searching questions. The rumors started to float around that a son-in-law of Patton's was involved in the mysterious affair in some way or other. A correspondent discovered by dint of much questioning that tough, swaggering Major Al Stiller, a conspicuous member of Patton's entourage, had disappeared. *Where had he gone to?* It didn't take the journalist long to find out that he had gone with the "raiding party." *But why?*

As Martin Blumenson put it much later:

Stiller's appearance and his presence with Baum's task force gave weight to the malicious gossip that circulated through the European theater after the war. His excuse for wanting to go along was obviously implausible.[1]

"Malicious gossip" or no, the correspondents' inquiries began to worry Patton. Some seven or eight days after the raid had ended he decided that he had better hold a press conference to explain his position, for as he confessed to General Bradley later, "he [Patton] was worried for fear that the newsmen might draw their own implications." And Bradley, who later wrote, "Certainly had George consulted me on the mission, I would have forbidden him to have gone ahead with it," agreed to the press conference.

Staged in the best Patton manner, it was a lie from start to finish. Displaying his personal diary, Patton denied that he had known his son-in-law Colonel Waters had been in the camp until escapees had reported the latter's presence to General Patch on April 4.[2] It was a lie he was

---

[1]It should be recalled that he had told a puzzled Baum that he was going along for the "thrills and the laughs."

[2]In his diary Colonel Codman, Patton's aide, records under the date April 4, 1945: "Later in the afternoon Gen. Patch called up to say that several escapees from the camp had arrived at his headquarters and reported that on its return trip the task force had been ambushed and overwhelmed . . . *From Gen. Patch, Gen. Patton learned that among the inmates of the camp was his own son-in-law Colonel John K. Waters*" [author's italics].

going to stick to for the rest of his life, and because even the hard-boiled correspondents did not believe that old Blood and Guts could run to such extravagant follies as to risk the lives of over three hundred men for the sake of his son-in-law's life, most of them were inclined to accept Patton's story. Hoge, Abrams and the Supreme Commander himself, General Eisenhower, kept their mouths shut—and were to continue to do so for over twenty years; the pressmen let themselves be appeased, and all that ever came out of that fateful interview which could well have destroyed Patton's brilliant reputation there and then, was a laconic, quarter-column report in *Time* magazine October 15, 1945, which read:

> Why did Patton order such a desperate undertaking [The Hammelburg raid]? One of the prisoners was Patton's son-in-law Lt. Col. J. K. Waters who was badly wounded in the fracas. Patton, denying that he ever knew Waters was there when he launched the operation, displayed his personal diary to prove it; his motive, he said, was concern for all Allied prisoners. Some men (including Hearst Correspondent Austin Lake, who was with the 3d Army at the time and told the story last week) *wondered if Patton should not have shown more concern for his own soldiers*[3] [author's italics].

And there it seemed that the Hammelburg affair had ended. Patton was now determined that no further news of the whole sorry business should leak out to the world at large. The two missing companies were quickly reorganized with replacements, to function once again as the 10th Infantry and the 37th Tank Battalions.

When thirty-five wounded members of Task Force Baum were recaptured at the liberation of the Hammelburg camp on April 6, they were speedily forwarded to Camp Lucky Strike in France and, in spite of the fact that a senatorial investigation committee would soon visit the repatriation camp for ex-kriegies because of the slowness of the repatriation process, *they* were shipped home immediately. Young Captain Baum was promoted major

---

[3] A "Major Baum" was quoted as saying that the operation had served a useful stragetic purpose.

and awarded the D.S.C. Later some critics were inclined to believe that although he well deserved the promotion and the medal, they were granted him so that he would keep his mouth shut.

Third Army spokesmen issued a laughable figure of the casualties incurred in the raid, which would be accepted uncritically by Koyen, the 4th Armored's historian, a few months after the war and continued to be accepted—equally uncritically—by anyone who has ever written about the affair (even by Toland, the first to reveal Patton's true motives in ordering the raid). In Captain Koyen's words: "Thirty-two of Baum's men were wounded, nine killed, sixteen missing in action."

And finally Patton clamped a strict censorship on any further mention of the incident, using, as an excuse presumably, the argument that the information might be of some use to the enemy.

From now on the Patton version of the Hammelburg raid was to be that it had been carried out in order to fool the enemy as to the intention of his main attack and that it had successfully confused the Germans at the price of but a handful of casualties. Yet when Patton gave the original order for the raid (which ran in a northeasterly direction to Hammelburg), he did not know the Supreme Commander's strategy for the remaining weeks of the war. In fact, on the very day that Baum took Oflag VII, Eisenhower issued his notorious stop-on-the-Elbe plan, which completely changed all previously held strategic concepts for the European theater of activities.

Nor it is likely that such a wily, skilled soldier as the German Commander in Chief in the West, Marshal Kesselring, would be fooled by Patton's "feint" (as Blumenson calls it); and even if he were, what difference would it have made? Blumenson says glibly that the "gossipers [i.e., Patton's critics] overlook the military reason for the action and the solid military accomplishment of the raid." What "solid military accomplishment"? Anyone who served in Germany that March knows well the total confusion of the enemy, hemmed in from west and east by a vastly superior Allied force, burdened by millions of refugees, paralyzed by Anglo-American air attacks. All the brave efforts of Baum's tiny force were but a drop in the bucket in the face of such mass confusion.

As for the "handful of casualties," one can only say that the official figure is ludicrously small. In the twenty-five years since the incident took place, the three writers who have concerned themselves with it (Koyen in 1945, Blumenson in 1955 and Toland ten years later) have all uncritically accepted the official figure. "This [the alleged confusion caused by the raid] a relatively small force had achieved at relatively small cost" writes Blumenson. Yet Baum himself told Koyen in 1945 that just before the last attack on Hill 427 "I could barely scrape together . . . two platoons, about 110 men."[4]

Writing twenty-five years later, General von Goeckel recalls the aftermath of the raid thus:

In the next few days the missing POWs started to return. Some came voluntarily and half starved from the woods in which they had been hiding; others were brought in by the farmers from the surrounding area. *Finally I had one hundred prisoners more than before the attack* [author's italics].

Now we know that only a handful of Baum's men and kriegies escaped to the Allied lines: the two lieutenants who got through to Patch's Seventh Army; Sergeant Graham of the 45th Division; others such as Staff Sergeant Kenneth Smith of "C" Company and Private First Class John J. McCarthy of "A" Company—perhaps a score in all, according to Koyen. If this is the case, what happened to the other hundred and sixty men—4th Armored or kriegies[5]—still unaccounted for? No one knows any more, for twenty-five years ago General George S. Patton

---

[4]In this figure might also be included the 65 or so kriegies who elected to go along with the task force. We have no way of knowing whether they were included.

[5]This figure is derived as follows: 20 survivors, say, who got through to the Allied lines; 25 killed or missing. These two figures plus the 100 mentioned by Goeckel make 145, leaving 160-odd missing out of the original 300-odd who set out on the night of March 26, or at least out of Baum's men and the kriegies who joined them.

was only too concerned to cover up the terrible wastage in human life and misery which his whim had occasioned.

Slowly the war drew to its close. In the second week of April, the 4th Armored Division's spectacular 500-mile gallop through Germany came to an end and it was ordered into reserve, never to fight again. General von Goeckel was captured and, after being treated well initially, was told by his American captors that General Patton had ordered his whole staff and finally himself hanged by the neck in a public square in Bamberg. When he asked why, his interrogator told him that he was suspected of slaughtering his prisoners at Hammelburg and a wooden door was brought in to prove "the case against him."

Goeckel looked at it curiously before his captor asked him if he recognized it.

The German said he did. It was from the hospital.

The American captain smiled grimly and pointed to the numerous bullet holes in it outlining the shape of a man. "And what are those?" he asked in German.

"Our camp doctor was a hunting fanatic," Goeckel explained.

"He used to pin the figure of a man to the door to do his target practice."

The American shook his head in disbelief.

Goeckel fought for breath. "If you don't believe me," he said firmly, "then let me know which of my prisoners are missing."

An hour later an American colonel appeared and told him that the charges against him had been dropped; none of his prisoners were unaccounted for.[6] Goeckel was taken off to a prisoner-of-war camp where he would remain for the next two years, this time experiencing camp life from the other side of the wire.

While Waters was being transported by ambulance and

---

[6] Today Goeckel believes that his former 'clients' had spoken on his behalf. I am inclined to believe him; all the former Hammelburg kriegies I have met have spoken highly of the German general.

then by plane back to hospital, Baum—in his usual independent manner—simply cadged a lift to the rear. It was typical of him. One morning, as Baum's wounds were mending in the 16th Evacuation Hospital, he nearly fell out of his bed. Coming through the swing doors and directly toward him was an unmistakable figure. Dressed in lacquered helmet, gleaming boots, his broad chest a blaze of ribbons, it was General George S. Patton!

Without too much ado and while his grinning staff looked on, he pinned the Distinguished Service Cross on a surprised Able Baum's pajama-clad chest. Baum looked up at the General, his eyes full of an unspoken question. The Hammelburg raid had been tagged as top secret. He figured that Patton would come in and give him the medal and then clear out. But Patton seemed to be hesitant about leaving.

Baum determined to stick his neck out, taking what he later called a "negative approach." "I'm sure, General," he remarked a little slyly, "you didn't send me to Hammelburg just to liberate your son-in-law.[7] As it worked out, our task force was a big diversionary maneuver." He hesitated while a somewhat puzzled Patton looked down at him on the hospital bed, probably wondering what was to come next. "The entire German corps, thinking the whole 4th Division was striking at Hammelburg, moved down to meet us."

He stopped abruptly and looked at the older man directly—almost challengingly.

Patton blinked. "Yes, it worked out very well," he said in that high-pitched voice of his. "Sorry we couldn't spare more troops for you."

Baum dropped the subject. He saw it wasn't welcome. After all, Patton was a four-star general and a very tough baby to boot. Instead, the two men talked about the role of tanks in warfare and the various types currently being used in the European theater of operations. Patton cited

---

[7] While in the Hammelburg POW camp hospital he had met Waters who (as Baum put it) "was completely disgusted" with the whole raid, its futility and the casualties it had caused among innocent men—so much that "he didn't even want to discuss it."

the "Long Tom" (the 240-cm. gun) as being the best tank weapon available.

Baum denied this. For him the best tank weapon was the tank itself.

Soon the brash young captain and the gray-haired general who commanded the destinies of 600,000 men completely forgot Hammelburg and quite an argument started. While Patton's aide—Codman—and the rest of the ward stared in amazement, the two men battled it out, with Baum, no respecter of rank, contending later that he had gotten the better of the argument.

Just before he left, a somewhat red-faced Patton asked, "Is there anything I can do for you, son?"

Baum jumped at the chance. "You certainly can, General. Get me out of this place and back to my outfit."

"You're forgetting the Geneva Convention, son," Patton replied.[8]

Baum looked up cheekily at the four-star general. "You're George S. Patton, aren't you?" he said.

Patton laughed. "All right, son, all right." He turned to Codman. "Get me the colonel in charge here."

A quarter of an hour later it was all fixed up. The hospital commander didn't like it, but Patton overruled him. Baum grinned; this was the second time he had discharged himself from hospital after being wounded!

As he went through the door, Patton turned and smiled admiringly at the wounded captain. "I'll get you a goddam plane," he chortled. Then: *"And give 'em hell."*

When Baum rejoined the 4th he was greeted as a ghost, a man who had risen from the dead. "I thought I got rid of you," Cohen cried happily, hugging him.

But the divisional surgeon was neither so happy nor enthusiastic. He took a quick glance at Baum and ordered him to rest. Baum insisted that he wanted to spend the remainder of his war with the battalion and, ignoring the surgeon, returned to the 10th. A day later, worried that he might have lost his nerve and be unable to lead men

---

[8]According to the Geneva Convention, a released prisoner of war could not fight in the theater of war in which he had been captured.

in combat, he went down to where one of the companies was dug in on the side of a river, facing the Germans. For forty-five minutes solid he exposed himself to a German artillery bombardment, with the shells falling by the score all around him. At the end of it he returned to battalion headquarters happy that his nerve hadn't gone.

The divisional surgeon was still less pleased when he heard of the latest Baum exploit. He called the divisional psychiatrist, with the amazing name of Earl Miracle, and told him, "Get that nut back to HQ in a hurry." Earl Miracle and the divisional surgeon, both buddies of Baum, insisted he had to take a rest, but he refused doggedly until General Hoge himself stepped in. Hoge told Baum severely, "I've got news for you. You're on the way to the Riviera."

When Miracle heard this, he gasped, "Maybe I made a mistake. *I should be so sick.*" Thus it happened that Baum was relaxing in the warm sun of the Riviera when the war ended.

Now the remaining Hammelburg kriegies were located, together with the survivors of the raid. They were imprisoned in the Moosberg POW camp. Soon they too would be released by Patton's men. Stiller was with them, ten pounds lighter and—according to Lieutenant Colonel Codman who drove to Moosberg to see him—"with ten dead Boches to his credit . . . and none the worse for his POW experience."[9]

And then suddenly the Hammelburg affair came to the forefront again, indirectly but decisively.

Sometime around April 11, two troopers of Patton's Third Army had been patrolling the streets of the small

---

[9]At Moosberg Camp, to which Patton himself went to inspect conditions, he first met the Russians, a contingent of whom marched out with (again according to Codman) "bearing, precision, staying power and discipline."

When Patton saw them, he said, "That's it. The Russian Infantry. Hard to beat." His eyes gleamed. "But it can be done and that is undoubtedly just what we shall have to do." It was one of the first of his anti-Russian statements which were soon to get him into serious trouble.

town of Merkers after curfew when they spotted a hurrying German woman. They stopped her at once, but she protested she was breaking curfew because she was going to the midwife for a neighbor. The two Americans decided to check her story—which turned out to be true—and in the course of the evening, as they passed the mouth of one of the salt mines of the region, the woman remarked, "That's the mine where the gold is buried."

The remark excited the men's curiosity and they made inquiries—with the help of a small charge of dynamite! They proved very fruitful. *They had discovered the entire gold reserve of the Third Reich!*

When the news of the gold reserve reached Patton, he ordered a censorship stop on the discovery. But the censor passed the story—*and, in addition, the story of the Hammelburg expedition,* one piece of news that Blood and Guts definitely did not want to reach the general public. Patton's reaction was typical. He fired the man, although he had no jurisdiction over him. The result was resentment at Public Relations Headquarters. As Captain Butcher, Eisenhower's all-important press aide put it: "Because of Patton's attitude, I knew that three or four correspondents had written bitter articles about him. Unfortunately they appeared as examples of 'Army blundering.'"

General Eisenhower, always conscious of his public image and perhaps even then thinking of his political future, decided to step in. He would have to talk seriously to "Georgie."

We do not know what Eisenhower said to Patton on that April 12 day when he visited the latter. Together with Generals Bradley and Eddy they went down the mine containing the gold in a primitive elevator, rattling with ever accelerating speed for two thousand feet down a pitch-black shaft. Patton, glancing up at the single cable that held them, cracked, "If that clothesline should part, promotion in the United States Army would be considerably stimulated."

Eisenhower answered, "O.K. George, that's enough. No more cracks until we are above ground again."

Later, after inspecting the hundred-million-dollars' worth of gold and the other precious things in the mine, Bradley, Eisenhower and Patton had dinner together during which Patton maintained he was unperturbed by the uproar caused by his sacking of the censor.

"I knew I was right on that one," he exclaimed, spearing a piece of steak.

"Well, I'll be damned," Eisenhower snapped. "Until you said that, maybe you were. But if you're that positive, then I'm sure you're wrong!"

Patton, supremely confident and at the height of his career, winked at the bespectacled General Bradley across the table.

"But why keep it a secret, George?" Bradley asked. "What would you do with all that money?" Bradley was puzzled, but then he still did not know his subordinate's other and more important reason for sacking the censor.

Patton chuckled, and then explained he would have the gold cut into medals—"one for every sonuvabitch in Third Army!"

Eisenhower, angry as he was with Patton, shook his head and, looking at Bradley, exclaimed, "He's always got an answer!"

But in spite of his comments, the dismissal of the SHAEF censor, over whom Patton had no authority whatsoever, infuriated Eisenhower. A few days later Butcher, thinking that his boss had not heard of the incident, brought it to Eisenhower's attention. He writes in his diary:

I told Ike of the flurry at PRD[10] amongst the censors because General Patton had arbitrarily fired one of them for passing stories that we had captured some of the German loot and of an expedition Patton had ordered to liberate some American prisoners.

He received as answer that Eisenhower had, in Butcher's words:

had this chapter and verse while he was visiting Patton and had made it clear to "Georgie" that he had no right to relieve a SHAEF censor . . . *Ike had taken Patton's hide off* [author's italics].

---

[10]Public Relations Department.

Butcher concluded by confessing ruefully that nonetheless, "I think Patton must have as many hides as a cat has lives, for this is at least the fourth time that General Ike has skinned his champion end runner."

But this time the good Commander Butcher was wrong in his assessment of his boss's attitude. The raid on the German POW camp and the sacking of the SHAEF censor marked a turning point in the Eisenhower-Patton relationship. In fact, Eisenhower, who had protected Patton so often in the past, felt that a baffling change had come over the man in the last few months that so blinded him to his glaring faults and his many shortcomings that he was beginning to make just too many blunders.

In his full-scale biography of Patton, Ladislas Farago maintains that from this time on:

> Eisenhower thought . . . something was driving him [Patton] into callous and arbitrary acts; he was arrogating undue privileges to himself; and he was behaving as if his natural place in history had filled him with reckless arrogance.[11]

When the war ended, Patton was given the command of Occupied Bavaria, but not for long. His anti-Russian remarks and his predilection for the conquered Germans did not endear him to Eisenhower. On the morning of September 22, 1945, at his first postwar press conference, he allowed himself to be quoted as saying: *"The American General Says Nazis Are Just Like Republicans and Democrats."* (This was the way the headlines of papers all over the States screamed the news the following day.)

Eisenhower reacted at once. He ordered Patton to retract the statement and to read a letter to the assembled press representatives on Allied policy to the defeated Germans. This Patton did, but he also read his own prepared statement, which said in part:

---

[11]It is interesting to note that although Farago interviewed Baum (according to his list of references at the back of his book) and twice mentions the name Hammelburg, he *does* not explain what took place there; the reader is left completely in the dark as to the nature of the event which got Patton into so much hot water. It is possible that Farago did not know about the incident. It is equally possible, however, that he thought any mention of it would damage the reputation of his hero.

I believe that I am responsible for the death of as many Germans as almost anyone, but I killed them in battle. I should be un-American if I did not try my uttermost to prevent unnecessary deaths after the war is over [he had just maintained he needed some Nazis in office to keep Bavaria from starving through the winter]. With the exception of these people, it is my opinion, to the best of my knowledge and belief, that there are no out-and-out Nazis in positions of importance . . .

When Eisenhower read the transcripts of the interview, he realized that Patton was either blind to the errors he had made or that he was simply not prepared to eat crow.

On September 28, 1945, Patton was summoned to Eisenhower's HQ in Frankfurt. There he was closeted with the Supreme Commander for two long hours while the bulk of the SHAEF accredited press corps waited eagerly outside. When he emerged Patton was pale-faced and shaken. Eisenhower had taken his beloved Third Army away from him!

Patton was to live two months more after that, in charge of a "paper army"—the Fifteenth, whose main job was to write the history of the war. November came and with it his 60th birthday. On that occasion he wrote: "It is rather sad to me to think that my last opportunity for earning my pay has passed." Now he contented himself with visiting the many liberated towns which wished to honor him, and with hunting.

Thus it was that on the morning of December 9, 1945, Patton, accompanied by his faithful aide General Gay, was driving along Highway 38 in the direction of the German town of Mannheim. They were on their way to a pheasant hunt in the woods close to the old imperial capital city of Speyer. Their driver was Pfc. Horace Woodring.

They were crossing the maze of railroad tracks on the northern outskirts of Mannheim, with Patton, as usual, dominating the conversation.

"How awful war is," commented the man who a year before had once said that war was man's greatest endeavor. "Look at all those derelict vehicles, Hap!" Then turning in the other direction, he exclaimed, "And look at that heap of rubbish!"

Involuntarily, the 23-year-old driver looked away from the road. It was at exactly that moment that a two-and-a-half truck, coming the other way, made a ninety-degree turn headed for a roadside quartermaster outfit.

Woodring saw it too late! Although he was going only thirty miles an hour, he slammed into the truck's gasoline tank. The sedan came to an abrupt halt.

In the first confusion, it seemed a minor accident. Woodring and Gay were shaken, but not hurt. Patton was bleeding from a cut in his forehead, but conscious.

"Are you hurt?" he was first to ask Gay.

"Not a bit, sir. Are you, General?"

"I think I'm paralyzed," Patton answered with that courage that no one—not even his bitterest enemy—could deny him. "I'm having trouble in breathing. Work my fingers for me, Hap."

The general did so several times, but when Patton said, "Go ahead, Hap, *work my fingers!*" he stopped and said simply, "I don't think it's advisable to move you, General."

Patton had broken his neck. He was paralyzed from the waist down.

Patton lay in the former little German hospital at Heidelberg for eleven days fighting for his life, while below, the minor fractures, the bleeding piles, the VD cases came and went. It was getter colder now. In the morning there was a hard white coating of hoarfrost on the ancient slate roofs of the old university city. On the anniversary of the day that Patton one year before had astounded a worried conference discussing the German breakthrough in the Ardennes with the brash statement: "Hell, let's have the guts to let the sons-of-bitches go all the way to Paris! Then we can really cut 'em off and chew 'em up!" Colonel Spurling, one of his doctors, knew that the crisis had arrived. A day later he announced that a blood clot had gotten loose in Patton's circulation, adding: "When a man is older, in bed and paralyzed, he's likely to get such a

clot in a vein of his leg or arm. It's always a great hazard
in the illness of older people . . ."

It seemed strange to many of his audience to think of
"Blood and Guts" as an *old* man!

Another day passed. In Germany and thousands of miles
away in the States, the half a million men who had once
fought under Patton's command prepared to celebrate
their first Christmas at peace after four years of war.

Epilogue

Most of the survivors of the Baum raid and the men they had rescued were home now. Graham, Nutto, Colonels Matthews and Lacey, young Hemingway—they were all free and beginning to prepare for a new life, away from the mud and misery of war and prison camp.[1] On that day, at exactly eleven minutes to six, the man who nine months before had altered all their lives one way or another died of acute heart failure when another blood clot struck his remaining lung. He died without a struggle and in his sleep. As the world's press headlined the news the following day, December 22, 1945: GENERAL PATTON DIES QUIETLY IN SLEEP.

The last ripple of the raid on Hammelburg Camp had come to rest. It was all over now.

"It is a great mistake to return to old battlefields," someone once wrote, "as it is to revisit the place of your honeymoon or the house where you grew up. For years you have owned them in your memory. When you go back,

---

[1] Young Abe Baum, 24 years old and well on his way to becoming a colonel as one of the most decorated men in the Army survived exactly two months in the Armored Training School. But as soon as he got his first taste of what the peacetime Army was going to be like, he got out. As he said later: he "preferred to pick [his] associates—not have them forced on [him]."

you find that the occupants have re-arranged the furniture."

The charred, reddened hull of the Sherman, surrounded by its silent little cluster of helmeted makeshift crosses which marked the graves of its crew, is no longer there. The long shell-pitted road, draped with white ribbons to indicate that the engineers had swept the verges clear of mines, which took a week to cover, can be walked now in a leisurely ten minutes. The squat ugly bunker, that held up a whole regiment for eight hours until a suicide squad of infantry, armed with bangelore torpedoes and flamethrowers, took it at the cost of fifty per cent casualties, is now simply a gentle mound, rather pretty in summer when it is covered with flowering wild roses.

Time, progress and the green earth itself have drawn an almost impenetrable cloak over those scenes of desperate action where young men fought, suffered and died a quarter of a century ago. In those once dreaded fields you left, littered with the rubbish of war—shattered tanks, abandoned equipment, the violently-done-to-death crumpled figures in khaki and gray—there are now only the gentle sounds and scents of the soft summer. So quiet, so innocent are those dark German fir woods, that even the most vivid personal recollections of the murder and mayhem that once took place in them finds the mind unwilling to accept the evidence of the map you carry and your memory. Suddenly you feel awkward at the thought that you are able to stand there at all—middle-aged and alive—in a position to look back; and there are moments of feeling that somehow you have broken faith when you stand alive in the place where young men, who once had laughed and joked with you, died.

But in spite of the quarter of a century that has passed since the bold raid on Hammelburg, the returning visitor can still find traces enough of that desperate dash so far behind the German lines. At Schweinheim—"Bazooka City" (as the GI's of the 4th Armored called it so long ago)—the half-timbered houses are still covered here and there with the ugly pockmarks of shrapnel and the odd, gouging wound of a Panzerfaust round. At Lohr, where the narrow country road starts to climb as it goes on to Gemünden, you can see—if you catch the light at the right angle—the line of shallow depressions in the lush green meadows where a salvo from Baum's Shermans rained down upon the surprised Germans.

Just outside Gemünden, where Baum halted and waited to hear if Lieutenant Nutto's men had taken the vital bridge, there is to the left of the road a simple hillside cemetery, *der Heldenfriedhof* (the heroes' cemetery) the Germans call it, in which a long line of soldiers' graves bears the date: 27.3.45. The ancient bridge, which Baum never took, has long since been repaired, but the span the enemy blew up, carrying with it the two GI's of the 10th Armored Infantry who pelted across it so desperately that long March day, is clearly more recent than the rest of the medieval structure; and the first man you speak to on the other side, just outside the station, was once a terrified ten-year-old boy in the church at Höllrich when those fanatical SS officer-cadets came stomping in to demand a tribute in blood from the Franconian peasants for having hoisted the white flags of surrender too prematurely.

Hammelburg itself is once more a camp: *Die Infantrieschule der Bundeswehr*—the West German Army's Infantry School. At the gate, with its familiar white and red striped pole of so long ago, you are met by a helmeted, pistol-carrying NCO who demands your business in precise, clipped military tones. You tell him and he shakes his head reluctantly. *"Amerikanische Kriegsgefangene? . . . Nein, nie gehört."*

He considers for a moment. "Now years ago, a crazy Ami turned up one day and said he had been in the place during the war. He had hidden some pearls in the camp. Could he try to find them again? Well, he convinced the camp *Kommandant* and they dug at the spot he had hidden. But they found nothing. *Garnichts*. If the pearls had ever been there, they had long since been found by some lucky soldier."[2]

---

[2] Who this American was, I have never been able to ascertain.

While he talks, your eyes wander. Then you spot them!

To the right of the gate *there are the huts!* Yellow and black with what look like imitation beams. (Later, when you wander around, you find the old stone building with the fading letters in old German Gothic script above the entrance—*Kommandantura*—this was von Goeckel's old headquarters.)

You ask the NCO about them. Again he shakes his wooden head. Stables, he thinks, from the old days when they had horses.

An officer arrives. The sergeant draws himself up. Clicking his heels, he salutes and explains the situation. The young officer shakes his head too. Slowly. *Kriegsgefangene?*

Natürlich, there are three prisoner-of-war cemeteries behind the camp, but they are from World War I. Would the gentleman like to see the camp's museum? Now that might be of interest?

The gentleman wouldn't, but he lets himself be persuaded. The museum is a couple of rooms, devoted to the history of the German infantry. It's a pathetic little place with a few exhibits—some dusty uniforms, a sand table with toy soldiers rushing stiffly and eternally up a hill, whose summit they will never reach, yellowed photographs of plump, bearded gentlemen in generals' uniforms. Not much at all.

The young officer apologizes. "It's difficult to get this sort of thing today. Naturally most people threw it away after"—he hesitates—"the war."

You nod your understanding and smile. He grows more confident. "But all the same, our young men who come here must be taught the advantages of a tradition—the tradition of the much maligned German infantry."

You mutter something or other and follow him out into the sunshine. And there is the tower. The water tower on which Baum's remaining Shermans wasted so much ammunition to so little purpose that March evening. And beyond it, across the flat parched fields which are now *Sperrgebiet*[2]—so the young officer tells you severely—and

---

[2] Restricted Area.

which echo the flat dry crack of the rifle and nervous chatter of the grease gun as the overweight teen-age German Army recruits practice for another war, rises the gentle wooded peak of the Reussenburg. Baum's Hill 427 —where it all ended so tragically and bloodily that bitter March night a quarter of a century ago.

Like that young German officer, General George Patton was also concerned with tradition. Once, in 1942, when he was comparing a group of new recruits he had just inspected with the doughboys he had commanded way back in World War I, he had thrown up his hands in that melodramatic way of his and exclaimed in apparent disgust, "We've pampered and confused our youth . . . Now we've got to try to make them attack and kill! *God help the United States!*"

Resting in his grave in that lonely mist-enshrouded cemetery just above the little capital city of Luxembourg, which he had once liberated, and surrounded by some 6,000 dead of his Third Army, Patton need not fear. The raid on Hammelburg which he so desperately tried to conceal from the American public, showed that the World War II GI had as much courage and dash as his predecessors of World War I. Or any war in America's history for that matter. The raid on Hammelburg deserves to be recognized as a worthy successor to Washington's raid on Trenton, or those of Stuart and Morgan in the Civil War, or the fight of the famous "Lost Battalion" in the Argonne in World War I.

General Patton was a man who starved for the super-patriotic rations of the melodramatic 19th century with dashing cavalry charges and "noble" deaths with a bullet through the heart. He was a mirror-gazing mystic who wrote poetry and believed in reincarnation. A "magnificent anachronism," as someone said of him. But he did not understand the modern, careless, undramatic GI, who could say of the general when he had become known by the nickname of "Old Blood and Guts": *"Yeah, his guts. Our Blood!"*

Thus it is not fitting that because one man, long dead,

had perhaps something to hide, the brave exploits of
Captain Baum's three hundred GI's of the 4th Armored
and the fighting kriegies they liberated should be forgotten
to history. Their story should be known in all its bravery
and tragedy, not as a warning in this age of Vietnam war-
weariness but as a memorial. Let us hope that this book
will help a little to set the record straight and serve as a
modest tribute to the courage of those young Americans
who died in a foreign field a quarter of a century ago.

And what of the survivors?

Some of them have died in the intervening years: Al
Stiller, going to the grave bearing his secret of the real
reasons for the raid; Pop Goode, as angry and pugnacious
as ever.

For the rest, they are today mostly steady, heavy-set
men advancing in years. Lieutenant Colonel Waters, for
instance, went on to realize that high promise which his
prewar career had predicted for him. In the fifties he
briefly commanded V Corps in Europe (which included
that division—the 4th—which had once so boldly tried to
rescue him). Sometime later he became chief of the U.S.
Military Mission in Yugoslavia, where he managed to
locate the Serbian doctor who had saved his life in Hammelburg, and to again thank him and bring gifts to his
family. Later still, in the early sixties, he was promoted to
four-star-general and made head of the Continental Defense Command before retiring from the Army.

General Hoge also retired from the Army, but he still
retained his aggressive energy, which had stood him in
such good stead in the Ardennes and at Remagen, and in
1969 he was again in Europe celebrating the 25th anniversary of the Normandy landings in which he played
such an important role.

General von Goeckel, in turn, survived two years of
internment on starvation rations while his wife subsisted
by selling goat's milk from door to door during Germany's
postwar black-market period. In 1970, aged 81, he is
retired in Bad Kissingen, a few miles away from the scene
of the raid.

Of the senior officers connected with the raid, however, it is Lieutenant Colonel Abrams who has made the biggest name for himself in the post-World War II scene. The burly, dynamic officer, who achieved such an outstanding record as a tank commander in Europe with the 4th Armored, went on to become a four-star-general and is, at the time of this writing, Commander in Chief in Vietnam.

Of the prisoners, some stayed in the Army, for instance young Lieutenant Jones, the son of the commander of the ill-fated 106th Infantry Division. He is presently a colonel in the Pentagon. Others left the Army, as did John "Bumby" Hemingway, who went into business, Lieutenant Colonel Matthews, who became a professor of economics, and Father Cavanaugh, who returned to a civilian parish.

And Captain Able Baum? The tall, rangy, tough leader of the raid went back to where he started—blouse-pattern cutting. Today he is in the same trade on Seventh Avenue in his native New York. The Army—perhaps understandably—no longer holds any glamor for him. "Sure it was rugged," he says now. "Another unit would have stopped and turned high tail. But we were soldiers. After all, we were the 4th Armored and in our outfit the unpardonable sin was to fail in a mission."

In 1945 Captain Baum's citation for the Distinguished Service Cross read:

> For extraordinary heroism in connection with military operations against an armed enemy in Germany . . . Despite his wounds he continued to lead the force throughout the day and following night until he was again wounded during an action on the outskirts of Hammelburg. Captain Baum's fearless determination and his inspiring leadership and loyal, courageous devotion to duty are in keeping with the highest traditions of the military service.

Reading that citation today, Abe Baum, one of the most decorated men in the "Fighting Fourth" with the D.S.C., four Purple Hearts, two Silver and two Bronze Stars, grins and says, "They gave me something to do and I took care of it."

It is as fitting an epilogue as any.

Bibliography

Ayer, Frederick, *Before the Colors Fade*. New York: Houghton Mifflin Co., 1964.

Blumenson, Martin, *The Hammelburg Affair*. (*Army*, 1965)

Blumenson, Martin, *Kasserine Pass*. New York: Houghton Mifflin Co., 1967.

Bradley, Omar Nelson, *A Soldier's Story*. New York: Henry Holt & Co., 1951.

Butcher, Harry Cecil, *My Three Years with Eisenhower*. New York: Simon and Schuster, 1946.

Codman, Charles, *Drive*. Boston: Little, Brown, 1957.

Farago, Ladislas, *Patton: Ordeal and Triumph*. New York: I. Obolensky, 1964.

Greger, Manfred, *Die letzten Kriegstage 1945 in Hammelburg*. Hammelburg: Stadtrat, 1965.

Keilig, Wolf, *Das deutsche Heer, 1939–1945*. Bad Nauheim: H.-H. Podzun, 1956.

Kesselring, Albert, *The Memoirs of Field-Marshal Kesselring*. London: W. Kimber, 1953.

Koyen, Kenneth A., *The Fourth Armored Division from the Beach to Bavaria*. Munich: Privately published, 1946.

Meyer, Robert Eugene, *The Stars and Stripes*. New York: D. McKay Co., 1960.

Murawski, Erich, *Der deutsche Wehrmachtbericht 1939–1944*. Boppard am Rhein: H. Boldt, 1962.

Patton, George Smith, *War as I Knew It*. New York: Houghton Mifflin Co., 1947.

Ryan, Cornelius, *The Last Battle*. New York: Simon & Schuster, 1966.

Schramm, Percy Ernest, *Kriegstagebuch des Oberkommandos der Wehrmacht 1940–1945*. Frankfurt: Bernard & Graefe, 1961–1965.

Toland, John, *The Last 100 Days*. New York: Random House, 1966.

Ullrich, Heinrich, *Chronik der Stadt Hammelburg*, Schneider & Co.

Wellard, James Howard, *General George S. Patton, Jr., Man Under Mars*. New York: Dodd, Mead & Co., 1946.

Wilmot, Chester, *The Struggle for Europe*. New York: Harper, c.1952.

Other Arrow Books of interest:

DEATH OF A DIVISION

Charles Whiting

They called it the ghost frontier . . .

December 1944. With the Germans in retreat, the 106th Allied Division were moved up to the frontier between Germany and Belgium. The war was apparently over on this frontier and they were the greenest division ever to be sent into the front line.

Within days, the 106th found themselves in the path of Von Manteuffel's mighty Panzer 5th Army – a quarter of a million men set on a last desperate offensive.

The 'Golden Lions' were trapped in one of the most disastrous miscalculations of the war – and the battle that followed was a frenzy of bloody chaos.

75p